Ghosts and Legends
of Charleston

Denise Roffe

4880 Lower Valley Road, Atglen, Pennsylvania 19310

Other Schiffer Books on Related Subjects:
Haunted Theaters of the Carolinas, 978-0-7643-3327-9, $14.99
Civil War Tours of the Low Country: Beaufort, Hilton Head, and Bluffton, South Carolina, 978-0-7643-2790-2, $16.95
Spirits of Georgia's Southern Crescent, 978-0-7643-2945-6, $12.99

Designed by "Sue"
Type set in Rosewood Std./NewBskvll BT
ISBN: 978-0-7643-3446-7
Printed in the United States of America

Schiffer Books are available at special discounts for bulk purchases for sales promotions or premiums. Special editions, including personalized covers, corporate imprints, and excerpts can be created in large quantities for special needs. For more information contact the publisher:

Published by Schiffer Publishing Ltd.
4880 Lower Valley Road
Atglen, PA 19310
Phone: (610) 593-1777; Fax: (610) 593-2002
E-mail: Info@schifferbooks.com

For the largest selection of fine reference books on this and related subjects, please visit our web site at:
www.schifferbooks.com
We are always looking for people to write books on new and related subjects. If you have an idea for a book please contact us at the above address.

This book may be purchased from the publisher.
Include $5.00 for shipping.
Please try your bookstore first.
You may write for a free catalog.

In Europe, Schiffer books are distributed by
Bushwood Books
6 Marksbury Ave.
Kew Gardens
Surrey TW9 4JF England
Phone: 44 (0) 20 8392 8585; Fax: 44 (0) 20 8392 9876
E-mail: info@bushwoodbooks.co.uk
Website: www.bushwoodbooks.co.uk

DEDICATION

To the owners of my heart:
My loving husband and my
beautiful daughter

ACKNOWLEDGMENTS

My heartfelt thanks go to the people of Charleston. They are the embodiment of genuine southern hospitality. I am honored to have met and interviewed those who have shared their stories with me and with my readers. I am blessed, too, to have met kindred spirits who have a penchant for historic research and a passion for the paranormal.

I would also like to thank all the members of Southeastern Institute of Paranormal Research: You have been inspirational, understanding, and the truest of friends.

I'd like to extend a special thank you to my husband, Danny, for his unconditional and unwavering love and support, and to my daughter, Meghan, for her patience and understanding and for not-so-gently nudging me when I needed it. I am the luckiest wife and mother on earth.

I would also like to extend a special thanks to the staff of Tumbleweed Southwest Grill in Dayton, Ohio who kept the chips and cheese dip coming as I wrote parts of this book during a necessary family trip and subsequent snowstorm.

CONTENTS

HOW IT BEGAN

Historically, field research of scientific inquiry into the unknown has been met with opposition. Over the last decade, though, the attitude toward those who embark on this endeavor has softened, in large part due to television shows like "Ghost Hunters" and "Paranormal State."

My personal interest in paranormal research was fostered by my mother's open mind and my father's attention to detail. I can remember him bringing home every book, and pointing out every article in the paper on paranormal events. Watching "In Search Of" was as much of a family event as watching "Little House on the Prairie" was. The lessons of both shows were discussed afterwards back in the days when family programming meant just that. On holidays, family gatherings during which my cousins and I spent time together were as likely to produce a séance as it was a game of hide-and-seek.

I've always been drawn to historic buildings and, of course, good ghost stories. But in all honesty I only began to use scientific equipment on investigations after the death of my mother in 1998. I had some personal experiences involving the spirit of my mom—and it was those experiences that led me to attempt to scientifically document spiritual activity.

Anatomy of an Investigation

Although I have been involved with various groups over the past eleven years, in September 2008 I co-founded my own research team with a friend, Diane Culpepper. Together with several of our closest, like-minded friends, we are the Southeastern Institute of Paranormal Research. There are several rules set forth for our team members that are designed to protect the integrity of our group, but also to protect any "evidence" that might be gathered during an investigation. The rules are simple and include:

† No smoking on the premises of the investigation's location.

† No wearing any cologne, aftershave, or perfume to an investigation.

† No partaking in alcoholic beverages within twenty-four hours of an investigation and using illegal drugs of any kind is strictly forbidden at any time — whether we're investigating or not.

† We also require annual background checks from all of our members.

If you're reading this and you suddenly start thinking that this sounds like something you would be interested in doing, there are a few things you should know. While conducting paranormal investigations can be a lot of fun, there is a lot of work to be done *before and after* actually setting foot on the premises of a reputedly "haunted" place — work that we, as investigators, are *never* paid to do. In fact, this is a costly endeavor. Beware too, that those who investigate evolve on a spiritual level. What once was a "hobby" will most likely grow into a very personal spiritual quest.

Whether we receive a phone call or seek out a location to investigate, the procedure is still the same. In either case, proper permission to investigate must be obtained. Property Managers do not own the property and therefore we need to seek permission from the owner(s). Once permission to investigate is granted, we will interview the current homeowners or witnesses to the phenomenon. This is followed by secondary interviews possibly with past homeowners or others who may have encountered strange events while visiting the location.

There is a basic set of questions that we use to interview our clients. In addition to understanding the activity that they are experiencing, it is important that we know whether or not our clients are on certain medications or whether they have been diagnosed with an illness. It is equally important to know the ages of all the members of the household and the religious orientation of our clients so that we can serve them well. Sometimes homeowners are reluctant to answer these questions as they can be a bit personal, but if we are to be of service, we truly need to know. This information is kept confidential.

Once we have completed the interviews, we will conduct historical research on the location. We may wait until after the initial investigation before conducting the historic background. This usually entails a visit to the local courthouse and historical or preservation society. The Internet is also a great place to find historical information on a specific location. Internet websites such as ancestry.com and findagrave.com are wonderful resources to help confirm dates of actual events. Most local newspaper archives can also be accessed via the Internet.

Prior to the investigation, Diane and I will visit the location. The reason for this is to get a layout of the property and the building or home. It is also so that we can have an idea of where to set up the equipment and get an idea of how many team members should be on location for the actual investigation. Once the interviews and initial visit are complete, the historical data is compiled and a date is set for the investigation.

We do not inform our team psychics/sensitives of any of the information concerning the property before the investigation. Instead, we bring them in "cold"; if it is a commercial property we are investigating, we normally have them meet us off the location somewhere so that they do not know where we are going before the investigation begins. In this way, we know that there is no way our psychics/sensitives could have prior information about the property or the ghostly goings-on. Of course, there are times when our efforts are in vain, as we have investigated many famous hauntings that our psychics/sensitives have heard of before. However, I'm always impressed with the details that they are able to relate.

On the night of the investigation, the team will meet at the appropriate time. After initial introduction to all the team members, our psychics/sensitives will stay in a "quarantined" area while the rest of the team is given a tour of the location. It's during this time that our technical team sets up the equipment.

Once the equipment has been set up and baseline readings obtained, the team will begin the investigation. The reason that we investigate in the dark is two-fold: Any photo/video anomalies will show up better with a dark background and human beings instinctively become quieter in a dark room as well. We typically investigate after dark because it is simply quieter at night.

The team will move throughout the location, pausing from time to time to conduct EVP sessions. EVP stands for Electronic Voice Phenomenon. This is the disembodied voice on an audio recording that was not present at the time the recording was made. The voice cannot be attributed to any team member or any other person who was present during the investigation.

The actual investigation consists of a lot of waiting around for something to happen. It is not a glamorous event. There are times, however, when things do happen and the team becomes excited. We have been trained to be wary of our reactions. I remember yelping at the sight of my first full-bodied apparition in the ladies lounge at Fox Theatre in Atlanta. It promptly disappeared. Since then I've been witness to several such sightings and regard them now much more casually.

After the investigation is when the real work begins. The team sifts through hours of audio and video recordings in search of any anomalies. Photographs are also carefully looked at. In the event that any anomalies are present, the team will first attempt to debunk it. In over eleven years of investigating, I have only seen three photographs taken by team members that I could not explain. One of them is included in this book. If there are anomalies that we cannot debunk, these are presented to the homeowner/property manager along with a detailed report that includes the historical data.

In the event that the team believes that "demonic" or negative activity is indeed happening at a particular location, we encourage the family to draw on their personal belief system and assist them in contacting clergy and counseling. Many teams offer "cleansings" to rid a home of negative energies. We do offer these services as well, but typically in conjunction with clergy and counseling for those bearing witness to the paranormal phenomenon. Everything we do is always at no cost to the homeowners/property managers.

About the Equipment

Those in the field of investigating the paranormal are at a disadvantage when it comes to the equipment that is available to us. The reason for this is simple. There is no proven scientific method for documenting paranormal activity. What we do use for investigations has evolved from trial and error while utilizing various pieces of equipment. The following is a basic list of equipment that we use on our investigations:

Electromagnetic Field (EMF) Meters: There are a variety of EMF meters that teams use while on investigations. We use tri-field meters as well as cell sensors and the infamous K-II meter.

Digital Camera: Used to capture photographic anomalies.

Digital Voice Recorders: Used to capture audio anomalies otherwise known as EVPs.

Electronic Voice Phenomenon (EVP): Unexpected sounds or voices that cannot be attributed to anything in the environment at the time of the recording. The classes of EVPs include:

> † Class A — The sounds are clear and loud.
>
> † Class B — The tones may be low. Usually the words are deciphered as having different meanings to different people.
>
> † Class C — The sounds or voices are extremely faint and difficult to decipher.
>
> † There are other classes that include Rev-A, Rev-B, and Rev-C: these are EVPs captured when the recording is played back in reverse.
>
> † The AVPs (Audible Voice Phenomena) are audio anomalies recorded that were *heard* at the time of the recording by one or more team members.

Infrasound Recorder: Used to capture audio anomalies in the lower frequencies of 1 to 20 Hz. This is of particular interest because human voices have been captured in this range, which is below the range of human hearing.

Various Video Cameras: All equipped with "night shot" and/or infrared lighting to help promote visibility in the dark.

Ambient Air Thermo Sensors: Documents temperature changes.

Thermal Cameras: Used to detect radiation in any given environment.

Since temperature causes variation in the amount of radiation emitted by any given object (or living thing), these variations are viewable with the camera even in a pitch-black environment.

ITC or Instrumental Transdimensional Communication: Recently there has been a wave in the invention and introduction of various devices that use radio frequencies as a means of capturing EVPs. "Frank's Box," otherwise known as the "Telephone to the Dead," and various "Radio Hacks" seem to be useful tools. They work by scanning various radio waves, which then allow spirits to put syllables together to form words and therefore communicate directly with the living. Along the same line is a device called an "Ovilus" that was invented by a man named Bill Chappell, who built and programmed this device with random words. The theory is like that of "Frank's Box" in that spirits can use syllables from various words to form other words that are not programmed into the device. While our team has yet to experiment with a Frank's Box, we have used several different radio hacks and our team member, Janet, does own an Ovilus. At this time, the Ovilus seems to produce more relevant words during investigations than the radio hacks. However, the team remains very skeptical of the process and it certainly can't be definitively proven that investigators are carrying on conversations with the dead.

The Definition of a Haunting

There is a consensus among paranormal investigators that several types of hauntings do occur. They are defined by the regularity in which they manifest as well as whether or not the energy is capable of seemingly intellectual interaction with the living.

Residual hauntings are the most common. They are the classic tales of the "lady in white" that mourns for her lover while walking the same path on the same night every year, or the Battle of Gettysburg that can be witnessed by intrepid onlookers. The theory is that intensely emotional events can leave an imprint on the space-time continuum. This imprint can then replay itself when the conditions are right, much in the same way a movie can be replayed from a recorder. Residual hauntings are also marked by the fact that the "ghosts" are not interacting with the living, but playing out a past event. Modern research suggests that witnesses are peeking into a time capsule and not necessarily witnessing a traditional ghost.

Poltergeist activity is what most people think of when they think about ghosts and hauntings. Typically this kind of activity is portrayed as objects being moved or thrown around a room and usually at one person in particular who is the focus of the haunting. Several theories have arisen concerning poltergeist activity. As research continues, investigators will attempt to answer the questions as to whether it is solely telekinetic energy being dispensed by an unwitting host or whether there is an actual ghost or spirit involved. Personally, I believe both scenarios are possible.

Traditional ghosts are those who have passed on, but are unaware that they are dead. At times they can be confused with residual energies. For example, Aunt Peggy can manifest in the living room sitting in her favorite chair crocheting a pair of slippers. A month later, she might tuck you in at night and give you a kiss on your cheek. In her reality, you may simply be in her home for a visit. It seems that traditional ghosts see only what they want to see and may be capable of intellectual interaction with the living.

Occasionally, I come across a haunting that is fascinating and baffling. While the word "demon" seems to be popular in the paranormal field today, I believe that there are other entities that can and do create spiritual and physical events that have never been in human form. There are also a lot of factors to be considered when dealing with what we believe to be a negative entity. It is not unusual to suggest counseling for clients who are struggling with this type of haunting. While several paranormal groups are prevalent across the country that like to say they specialize in demonic exorcism, I find that those particular spiritual cleansings are better left up to the experts. Too many times I've seen well-meaning researchers end up being the target of negative attacks and in dire need of spiritual help themselves.

Spirit visitations are very common as well and my favorite to investigate. Usually (but not always), the spirit is a family member or other close loved one coming with a message for the person (or people) experiencing the haunting. There are several ways in which we attempt to communicate with the spirits and help them to get their message to their loved ones. It is not uncommon for psychics to deliver messages to loved ones from the dearly departed. However, the family member usually has an inkling of what the message is once they realize there's no reason to fear the "ghost."

So what is it that causes some places to ooze with ghostly phenomenon? If you were to pose that question to a hundred paranormal investigators, you would likely get a hundred different responses. All that I can offer are my own theories based on the research that I've developed over the past eleven years. Old creaky buildings and land with a rich history seem to offer up more phenomena than the brand new home built in a modern-day subdivision. As an investigator, I have asked myself why and continue on my quest to find an answer. It seems logical to me that the more living, breathing people that have experienced life in a particular location, the more energized the location becomes and therefore the more paranormally active an area might become.

WHY CHARLESTON?

Charleston has no lack of documented history. The city seems to breathe as one walks along the cobblestone streets. English settlers founded Charles Town in 1670 on the west bank of the Ashley River. By 1680 the settlement had grown and moved to the peninsula where it exists today.

The settlement was often the focus of attacks from Spain and France, which contested England's claim to the colony. Native Americans and Pirate raids added to the misery of Charles Town citizens. In response, the colonists erected a fortification wall around the small settlement. Only two buildings remain today of that original settlement: the powder magazine, where the city's gunpowder was stored, and the pink house, which is believed to have been a colonial tavern.

Charleston has been dubbed the "Holy City" due to the many churches that dot its skyline. One of the oldest churches that still survive today is St. Michael's Episcopal Church. The cornerstone was laid in 1752 and the church opened in 1761. Refugees from France

One of the oldest buildings in Charleston is the Powder Magazine, circa 1713.

The only remaining independent Huguenot Church in America.

founded the French Huguenot Church in 1681. The first Huguenot Church was built on the site in 1687. That building was destroyed in a 1796 fire; the building that stands today was built in 1845 and remains the only independent Huguenot Church in America.

Charleston is a city steeped in history. Through fires, earthquakes, wars, and piracy... it has withstood the test of time. Stories of tragedy and triumph are abundant throughout the city, but in the shadows and down cobblestone avenues lurk mysterious echoes from the past. The following stories have been relayed to me by people who have experienced ghostly activity in the Holy City. Most of the stories are first hand accounts and others are ghostly legends that have been passed down through generations. Some of the names have been changed at the request of those who were kind enough to share their stories, however, wish to remain anonymous.

Chapter One:

CHARLESTON'S HAUNTED HISTORY

60 Seconds...

Most of us will never comprehend how sixty seconds can change our lives forever. It is literally in these moments when tragedy strikes that define us and give our lives meaning...or conquer us and leave us empty shells of what we could aspire to become.

THE 1886 EARTHQUAKE

August 31, 1886 was a typical hot southern day. Even the trade winds blowing off the ocean didn't quite seem to reach the inner parts of Charleston. The night air was unusually balmy and still. Gas lamps graced the streets... the lamp-lit streets were safe and the pleasant glow was warm and welcoming to weary, tired seafarers.

Charleston residents were going about their daily routines when, at 9:50 p.m., the city began to shake. By the time it stopped shaking at 9:51 p.m. — a mere sixty seconds later — scores of South Carolina residents were dead and more than six million dollars worth of damage to historic structures remained. The people of Charleston gathered outside in the parks and common areas setting up makeshift tents and tending to the injured and dying. Shock settled in and created havoc as some began to ramble and wander the streets aimlessly. Some of them were never seen again.

Cora's Tale...

Cora had finished her evening chores and retired to her bedroom. Her mother had passed away in childbirth years earlier when Cora was very young. Cora and her father had moved to Charleston and settled into a comfortable residence near East Battery Street. While

Cora slept, her father retired to the library where he was reading by candlelight.

Cora didn't know what was happening. At first, she thought she was dreaming. In the dark, she heard the chimney fall from the roof causing a terrible crash. She ran down the stairs and called out to her father. He grabbed her and together they ran outside and crossed the street to an open park where they stood with their neighbors. The ground had stopped trembling, but several small fires were now raging throughout the city. Each dwindling aftershock renewed their terror.

The ocean seemed to billow wildly and crashing waves could be heard over the chaos. As more residents gathered in the park, some of them injured and dying, Cora and her father gathered materials and helped to build makeshift tents.

Elizabeth's Tale

In Summerville, just twenty-six miles outside Charleston, Elizabeth was cradling a sick baby. John, her husband, had traveled toward Charleston to seek medicine for the ailing infant, who had been battling a fever for several days. Elizabeth was praying when the earthquake struck and at first thought that God had come down to answer her prayer. When the walls began to crumble, she ran outside to the open field, clutching her sick child. After finding a safe place to sit down, Elizabeth prayed harder.

Cora's Tale

In Charleston, Cora's father instructed her to stay at the park before leaving with several other men in an attempt to extinguish the growing flames popping up all around the city. She banded together with the other women and forced herself to focus on the task at hand. Together, she and the women made makeshift cots and tended to the injured and dying. Cut off from the outside world — as the telegraph wires were also destroyed — wild speculation ran rampant. The theory that seemed to stand up to all logical reasoning was that the southern states must have split from the nation and was now adrift on the ocean. Panic was widespread and Cora knew that she had to work with the other women to help keep her neighbors calm.

Elizabeth's Tale

Back in Summerville, it had been several hours since Elizabeth first fled into the field. Although the ground had stopped shaking, she was afraid to re-enter the house. She quietly gathered some tall grasses and made a makeshift bed, wondering if her husband had experienced the earth shaking and whether or not he was okay. The baby was sleeping now. Elizabeth cradled the tiny infant in her arms as she drifted off to sleep, tortured by thoughts of what the future held for her and her family.

Cora's Tale

In the park, Cora was working feverishly, tearing cloth to make bandages. The injured seemed to pour into the makeshift tents. She was tired — and worried. Her father had not yet returned. Tears welled up in her eyes as she fought off panic. When someone began to sing, Cora joined in and soon her tears were replaced by a blind determination. Sunrise would come and she would find her father safe and sound.

Sunlight shines through the branches of a Charleston oak tree.

Elizabeth's Tale

A sleeping Elizabeth stirred as the baby began to coo. When she opened her eyes, a faint orange glow was illuminating the field. Elizabeth looked down to see the smiling face of her baby girl. She was stunned to realize that the baby's fever was gone — God had answered her prayers.

Elizabeth then lifted her gaze toward the house and she saw a woman standing a few feet away. The woman was wearing a blue dress and was surrounded by a bright golden light. Her skin seemed to glow as well and, as Elizabeth watched her, the woman smiled. Elizabeth was overcome with a sense of peace as she watched the apparition disappear before her eyes...

Through the foggy remnants, she saw the faint outline of a man. As her eyes focused, she realized the form was her husband crossing the field from what was left of their house. As he called out to her, Elizabeth stood, holding the happy, tiny infant. Her husband ran to greet her.

Cora's Tale

By morning, a determined Cora was standing in the street. She had begun to search for her father. Her nightgown was covered in blood. Her head and her hands ached. The tears she was able to keep at bay throughout most of the night were flowing freely now. She sat on the steps of a building and, feeling lost, held her head in her hands.

When she heard a woman calling her name, she lifted her eyes toward the sound of the sweet voice. A few feet from the steps where Cora was sitting, a woman offered her an outstretched hand. She was wearing a blue dress and Cora silently wondered why the woman was so clean and presentable. Could it all have been a dream? Behind the apparition, the morning sun was illuminating the woman's hair. Cora was transfixed as she noticed that the woman was translucent and glowing. Believing that she had somehow died and that this woman was an angel to take her to heaven, Cora stood to take her outstretched hand.

A block away, a man began to run in her direction, as he recognized his daughter, shouting her name. As Cora heard her father's voice, she realized that she wasn't dead after all and the glowing blue angel disappeared. Cora ran to her father and fell into his arms. The two walked back to their damaged home with a renewed sense of what was most precious.

One Angel, Two Women

Some years later, after Elizabeth and her family moved to Charleston, she met Cora at a picnic. As the day wore on, talk revolved around the great earthquake of 1886. Cora and Elizabeth soon realized they had seen the same angelic apparition and remained close friends until Elizabeth's death in 1901.

THE OLD JAIL

Because of the many apparitions reported here, Bulldog Tours began offering exclusive tours in the building more than three years ago. Tour guide Suzann Brown has a book coming out about the Old City Jail. This is one Charleston location where the historical facts may be just as intriguing as its current ghostly residents. If you would like to visit the Old City Jail, be sure to book a tour with Bulldog Tours. Visit their website at www.bulldogtours.com or contact them at 843-722-8687.

Its History

At the corner of Logan and Magazine streets stands what appears at first glance to be a castle. The Old City Jail was constructed in 1802 and was in use until 1939. Reminiscent of eighteenth century castles in Europe, there is a famous "lady in white" that frequently walks the yard and nearby neighborhoods searching for a husband. She is only one of many apparitions that are seen here.

Construction of the Old City Jail began in 1790 on top of a burial ground that interred indigents, African-Americans, and those who could not be identified from 1742 until 1780. Daniel Duncan, a very young black man, was the last prisoner hanged there in 1911. He was convicted of murdering a shop owner, though many Charlestonians believe Duncan was innocent. He reportedly hanged for thirty-nine minutes until he died, in effect strangling to death.

Old City Jail, circa 1802.

The Legend of John and Lavinia Fisher

The legend of how John and Lavinia Fisher came to be incarcerated at the Old City Jail developed over more than a century ago. Generations passed down the story to their children and, with each telling of the tale, more embellishments were added. My friend and SIPR team member Amanda calls this the "multi-generational telephone game."

In the early 1800s, there were several inns located on the outskirts of Charleston. In fact, from the documents that are available today, we know that there was the Four Mile House, Five Mile House, and the Six Mile Wayfarer's Inn. These inns were located on the mail route and the main thoroughfare that led into downtown Charleston. Eventually, those who traveled the route were targeted by groups of criminals and highway robbers. Everyone who passed by was subject to robbery and some say murder was not uncommon.

The legend states that John and Lavinia Fisher owned Six Mile Wayfarer's Inn. However, instead of providing a place of refuge, they would take in weary travelers only to poison them with oleander tea. Once they had retired to their quarters and fell asleep or slipped into a coma, John would turn a crank that flipped the mattress over and the unsuspecting guest would be tossed into a pit beneath the bed. There he would languish until the poison took his life. John and Lavinia would take all of their guest's possessions including their horses and these items could then be sold for quite a handsome profit.

Lavinia was a woman of legendary beauty. Her long dark hair and remarkable features were captivating. When Lavinia was confronted with a conviction, she reminded the judge that she could not be executed because she was a married woman. The judge was quick to remedy that and simply hanged John first. Lavinia was now a widow.

On a cold February morning in 1820, Lavinia Fisher was placed in the jail paddy wagon and paraded through the cobblestone streets of Charleston. This was the normal practice of the day, but what wasn't so normal was that Lavinia was dressed in an elegant bridal gown. As she was paraded through the streets, she called out

The Old Paddy Wagon escorted the beautiful Lavinia to her final destination.

to the masses for someone to save her, hoping that her captivating beauty would seduce someone into marrying her. It didn't work and Lavinia was hanged.

Fact vs. Fiction

The true story of what happened to John and Lavinia is much more compelling. Several accounts of missing merchants and family members were made to the Sheriff's Department. However, a lack of evidence made an official investigation into the matter impossible. The good citizens of Charleston became impatient with the criminal activity along the route and, after a discussion with local authorities, a group of thirty men headed out to dissolve the band of highway robbers who were using the inns as their headquarters.

The men stopped first at Five Mile House. There, they surrounded the residence and informed the occupants that they had fifteen minutes to pack and leave. The gang of criminals held up inside responded to this by firing their weapons at the mob. The mob responded by burning down Five Mile House and the outbuildings. The criminals fled into the woods.

The mob of men then moved on to Six Mile Wayfarer's Inn, where they repeated the process. However, instead of resisting, John and Lavinia Fisher, along with their gang, abandoned the property. The mob of men left one man in charge at the inn. His name was Dave Ross.

Mr. Ross spent one night at the inn. In the morning, he was confronted by a man named William Heyward, who had returned to the house with John and Lavinia Fisher. Heyward insisted that Mr. Ross leave the premises. When he protested, he was beaten. Turning to Lavinia for help, he was shocked when she instead put her hands around his neck and began to choke him. She then thrust his head through a glass window. David Ross, bleeding and scared, fled the scene on his horse and immediately made his way to Charleston and the authorities.

Meanwhile, a merchant named John Peoples stopped by Six Mile Inn to water his horses on the way back to his home in Georgia. At the well, he found a young boy filling up a bucket. According to his affidavit, a "drunken man" came out of the house and insisted that the young boy give him the bucket. When the man made a move toward the child, Mr. Peoples "cracked" his whip toward the man. This incited rage and it wasn't long before there were many people flowing from the inn, all carrying pistols, knives, and clubs. Mr. Peoples was attacked. When the attack was over, he had been robbed. Broke and beaten, Mr. Peoples headed to the police in Charleston. When he arrived, he found Mr. Ross filing his affidavit.

The Charleston Police wasted no time returning to the inn. There, they found the skeletal remains of at least two former guests. That was enough to arrest John and Lavinia Fisher, along with several of their "staff." The group was taken to the Old City Jail.

John and Lavinia Fisher are said to have been imprisoned together in a 6' x 8' cell on the third floor. They eventually planned and executed an escape attempt with another inmate. However, the plan failed when the rope that they had fashioned from bed sheets broke before Lavinia could escape. John and the other inmate were recaptured the next day.

John and Lavinia Fisher were hanged together on February 18, 1820. The gallows stood at where Meeting Street Road met the Cooper River Bridge. There is no record that Lavinia was wearing a wedding gown. Her last words were: "If you have a message for hell — give it to me. I'll carry it."

According to Suzann Brown of Bulldog Tours, newspapers at the time reported more than 1,100 people attended Lavinia and John's executions. Lavinia has the dubious distinction of being the first female serial killer in the history of the United States.

Many people claim to have seen the ghostly apparition of Lavinia in and around the jail throughout the years. The Six Mile Inn was burned to the ground after the executions at the order of the Chief of Police of Charleston. The scorched remains were visible for years even after a new Inn was built on the same lot. Today, neither of the inns exist any longer.

Denmark Vesey

On a cool fall evening, Sarah and her friends were walking along Magazine Street. They had started out walking down Broad Street near the hotel and ventured a couple blocks north before finding themselves in front of the Old City Jail. They stopped to read the plaque on the front of the building and then walked around the back, following the fence. As they stood gazing at the old paddy wagon still on the property, the girls began to chat about how the conditions must have been at the Old City Jail. Sarah glimpsed a black man standing near the paddy wagon. He was well dressed in a clean white shirt and black overcoat. As she watched him, Sarah became alarmed... the man was floating just above the ground.

Local legend states that Denmark Vesey was brought to the Old City Jail in 1822 after being accused of conspiring to start an uprising of South Carolina slaves. He was reportedly kept in the upper tower. Newspaper articles of the time indicate that rumors of a slave rebellion began when a young slave told his master that Denmark Vesey was encouraging thoughts of freedom. The plot that Denmark Vesey was accused of entailed the simultaneous uprising of slaves across South Carolina and up the coast to murder their owners and seize the city of Charleston. Denmark and his followers then planned on sailing to Haiti to escape prosecution.

In all, 130 men were arrested and charged with conspiracy; sixty-nine of those were convicted and eventually thirty-five were hanged. Of the remaining convicted, twelve had their sentences commuted, twenty-one were deported, and one was ordered to leave the state of South Carolina, but could remain in the United States. Of the sixty-one who were acquitted, nine were remanded to their masters under the condition that they be transported out of the country without trial, twenty-seven were discharged by the court, and twenty-five were discharged by the Committee of Vigilance. ("The Projected Servile Insurrection at Charleston, SC," New York Herald, December 1, 1859.)

Denmark was purchased in 1781 by Captain Joseph Vesey in St. Thomas. After a brief stay in what is now Haiti, Denmark was brought into Charleston, where he was kept as a domestic slave. On November 9, 1799, he won a local lottery of $1,500. With that, he bought his freedom and began working as a carpenter. Denmark eventually co-founded a branch of the African Methodist Episcopal Church in 1816.

One of Denmark's best friends, Rolla Bennett, was instrumental in Denmark's conviction. He committed suicide knowing that his testimony sent his friend to the gallows. Although the exact spot where Denmark — as well as John and Lavinia Fisher — was hanged is unknown, some say he has never left the Old City Jail. His apparition has also been seen wandering the grounds near his home at 56 Bull Street.

Historic records indicate that the main gallows was originally located where the Old Exchange and Provost Dungeon are today. However, we know that the area now known as White Point Gardens was also used for hangings. Another historic record indicated hangings at various other smaller unnamed locations. Also unknown is the place where Denmark and the Fishers were interred. Historic documents only indicate a "potter's field."

Several years ago there was a woman tending her garden at the corner of Bee and Ashley Streets. While she was digging, she discovered human skeletal remains. Historic records indicate that the property was once a "potter's field" or "pauper's field" as early as the 1700s. Later the site was used for the Porter Military Academy. Although there were several potter's fields located throughout Charleston, this particular location is of interest because historic documents state that hanged criminals were interred here.

When the Medical University of South Carolina Children's Hospital broke ground there, more skeletal remains were discovered. The remains were cremated and scattered in the place where they were found. Today, a plaque on the MUSC campus sidewalk, between the Waring Historical Library and the Macaulay Museum of Dental History, commemorates the unknown who are interred underfoot.

A True Ghost Tour

Tour guides and guests alike have relayed their experiences in the Old City Jail. When I met with Ginger Williams of Bulldog Tours, I asked her if she had personally experienced anything in the building. She said that sometimes when she is on the third floor, she would hear footsteps on the fourth floor going across and above her. What's wrong with that? There is no fourth floor at the Old City Jail any longer and no one else is ever in the building at the time. Ginger also said that once she was on the third floor, she was standing approximately six feet from the window. There was a brick on the windowsill that inexplicably flew out and landed just beside her foot.

On the third floor of the Old City Jail, there is also a room shaped like an octagon. Once Ginger was in the octagon room with some ghost hunters conducting an EVP session and, as they began, a set of bars that was leaning up against the wall began to rock and then slid down the wall. The bars were very heavy and made of iron. It took two people to move the iron bars in an attempt to debunk what they had just witnessed. There was a deep gauge in the wall left by the heavy moving bars. Ginger also added that while on a tour last year she saw a glowing skull drifting out of a room with red rings of light around it. At first she thought that maybe she had imagined it...until one of the guests standing behind her mentioned seeing the same thing.

Suzann Brown has developed her own approach to guiding tours through the building. Both a spiritual person and a gifted sensitive, Suzann stated that she prays for peace and protection each night before she enters the building. On one such night, she walked up the stairs and entered through a back door. As was her usual routine, she lit candles in the windows on opposite sides of the door where tour customers would normally enter to begin the tour. On this night, as she stood in the glow of the candlelight in the silent building, a feeling of uneasiness surrounded her. It was then that both candles blew out. After attempting to relight the candles a second time, she spoke aloud to whatever was demanding her attention. The candles blew out again. She explained what she was doing there and that visitors would be in the Old City Jail on that night. When she made the third attempt, the flames grew and didn't go out again.

Another tour guide stopped by the Old City Jail on a sunny spring afternoon. She was on the second floor when she heard a noise coming from below. She made her way to the basement to what was once the kitchen area. As she entered the room where food was once delivered and prepared, she noticed a mist. As she turned to leave, the mist seemed to take the form of a man. She stood, transfixed, as the apparition went about preparing an invisible meal.

From Suzann Brown's booklet "A Brief History Revealed, The Old City Jail & Prison Camp of Charleston, South Carolina":

> "Meals for the prisoners would be prepared by inmates known as trustees in the kitchen located in the basement area on the western side of the jail. Watered down soups, stews, 6-9 ounces of bread were served to the prisoners out in the jail yard or by means of a dumb-waiter located in the Holding Cell building. Large kettles of food would be placed on a sturdy wooden platform in the kitchen and a cable system carried the food up a four-story shaft to the upper floors. Whether the meals were available once a day or three times a day is unknown, however, the long-standing hanging day meal was supposedly a serving of eggs, meat, bread, and milk. The practice of withholding food and/or water was often used as a form of torture during the Old City Jail's existence."

The Mysterious Keys

Suzann and Ginger have been tour guides at the Old City Jail for years. Both women have described paranormal activity around the area where the old iron keys are on display. It seems there is an entity that doesn't like anyone to touch the jail keys. Curious tour customers have been known to jingle the keys in an attempt to provoke a reaction from "the warden." The temperature has been known to drop significantly and ghostly footsteps can be heard as a

The Warden's Keys... The author had her own paranormal experience with them.

shadow person darts from room to room.

On one of my visits to the Old City Jail, I was drawn to the area where the old keys were displayed on a wall. I was truly fascinated, thinking of all the prisoners that had been locked in the old jail and how many times the keys might have turned a lock, granting freedom to one of the convicts. As I turned to walk down the stairs, I heard the unmistakable sound of old metal clanking against the wall. I turned back in time to see the two hundred-year-old keys swaying.

THOMAS ROSE HOUSE

A young mother walked up the stairs to the third floor of a private residence on Church Street and tucked in her two small children in separate bedrooms. As they were new to the house, the children were disquieted and kept calling their mother back and forth between the rooms for comfort and one last drink of water...and just one more bedtime story.

It was during one of these trips between bedrooms that the young mother paused. She sensed something or someone on the stairs. From the corner of her eye, she saw the figure of a man. She turned and he stood staring at her from the landing. He was dressed in eighteenth century clothing and disappeared before the young mother could speak to him.

In 1680, the land where the Thomas Rose House now stands was deeded to Elizabeth Willis. In 1701, the land was deeded to William Elliott and then to his son, Thomas Elliott. The beautiful house, which stands today at 59 Church Street, was built by Thomas Rose after his marriage to Beuler Elliott, the daughter of Thomas Elliott, in 1733. By 1783, the house was occupied by Fannie and Dellie Rose, great-granddaughters of Thomas Rose.

In 1783, a young man rode in a stagecoach staring out the window remembering his first meeting with his true love in Newport, Rhode Island. She was in the library and they struck up a conversation about poetry when she was searching for Spenser's Fairie Queene. He fondly recalled her blonde hair and the way her crystal blue eyes shined as they spoke. The following day he found himself in the parlor

The Thomas Rose House is a private residence.

THOMAS ROSE'S HOUSE

c 1735

In 1680, Town Lot No. 61 was granted
by the Lords Proprietors to Elizabeth Willis,
and in 1701 was deeded to William Elliott
and later to his son, Thomas Elliott.
This notable early Georgian house
replaced a smaller house on the premises,
and was built by Thomas Rose
soon after his marriage in 1733 to
Beuler Elliott, daughter of Thomas Elliott.
In 1786, Doctor Joseph Ladd Brown
was carried to his room in this house
after being mortally wounded in a duel.
It is alleged that his ghost still inhabits the house.

placed by

THE PRESERVATION SOCIETY OF CHARLESTON

THIS PROPERTY HAS BEEN
PLACED ON THE

NATIONAL REGISTER
OF HISTORIC PLACES

BY THE UNITED STATES
DEPARTMENT OF THE INTERIOR

of her home sharing his own poetry. Many more visits followed that first encounter and before long Joseph Ladd Brown and Amanda were engaged, albeit in secret. Amanda was an orphan placed in the care of relatives. They had refused every offer for her hand, knowing that with her wedding they lost the management of her fortune.

Having spent four years as an apprentice with Dr. Senter in Rhode Island, the young man was now Dr. Joseph Ladd Brown. Eager to establish his career and earn the hand of his beloved Amanda in marriage, he heeded the advice of Revolutionary War hero and friend of his father, General Greene, and traveled to Charleston to establish his profession.

The legend states that his stagecoach stopped at a tavern on the outskirts of town. A young Dr. Brown climbed down and stood on the cobblestone street taking in the evening air. It was there that he met Ralph Isaacs and the two became fast friends.

Soon after his arrival in town, Dr. Brown took a letter that he had carried from General Greene to the dear ladies who resided at the Thomas Rose House. The ladies offered him room and board, and so the young doctor moved into the Church Street residence the following day.

On a cool fall evening in 1786, Dr. Brown walked down the street to attend a theatrical performance. By the end of the evening, Dr. Brown and his friend Ralph Isaacs were arguing about the talents (or lack of talent) of a particularly beautiful actress that performed on stage that night. Eventually Isaacs challenged Dr. Brown to a duel.

The following morning Dr. Brown's anger had subsided enough that he didn't want to injure his friend and fired his pistol "wide off his mark." Apparently Isaacs was still quite angry, but didn't want to kill Dr. Brown either and fired his pistol, striking the young doctor in his knee. Dr. Brown was carried into the house where he developed gangrene and died three weeks later. His beloved Amanda received the news in Rhode Island of his passing before she could make the trip to Charleston. Numerous reports of a spectral figure resembling Dr. Brown have been made over the years around the Thomas Rose House. Another account comes from a visitor to the house many years ago:

She was reading before going to bed in one of the second floor bedrooms when she heard the unmistakable sound of a man whistling. Knowing there were no men in the house aside from her husband who was sleeping in the bed next to her, she opened the bedroom door and carefully stepped into the dimly lit hallway. The pleasant sound of whistling and voices carried down the hallway.

She stated, "I wasn't frightened by the sound, but puzzled. It sounded like a party was going on and the whistler was very jolly."

As she turned to return to her bedroom, she caught a glimpse of a man walking toward her and described him as "translucent and whistling. He continued down the stairs as though he was unaware of me."

Present Day

I called the current owner, Cathy Forrester, and she agreed to meet with me. I arrived on a sunny afternoon with friends in tow. After brief introductions, Ms. Forrester was gracious in giving us a tour of the beautiful home. We sat in the front parlor and discussed the paranormal events that had been reported. Ms. Forrester said that her parents bought the home in 1941 and that after their death, she and her family moved into the home in 1988. She had never really encountered anything frightening in the home, but knew of the stories and welcomed our skeptical input.

The ghostly apparition of a child has also been seen in the garden at the Thomas Rose House. It is rumored that the body of a child is interred in the corner of the garden. However, no formal documentation could be found to back up the rumor. Cathy Forrester has written a wonderful book about her life in Charleston and the Thomas Rose House. Be sure to visit her website at www.athomecharleston.com.

CHARLESTON LIBRARY SOCIETY

There are three buildings side by side that house the Charleston Library Society, founded in 1748. The main building was built between 1912 and 1914. The Barnwell Annex was once a home and now holds the library's video and audio collection. The newest building was built in 1996.

The Charleston Library Society... Does the apparition of William Hinson roam the halls?

A Roaming Spirit

A library employee (who wished to remain anonymous) walked through the back door on a cool morning several years ago and stopped in her tracks. Standing at the end of a table across the room was a man. When the "fight or flight" reflex kicked in, she stood motionless. It was then that she realized that the man seemed to be from another time. He was wearing a dark coat and a hairstyle indicative of an earlier period. He was not in silhouette, nor was he translucent. He appeared to be solid...until he vanished.

Another employee, Janet, has been working at the library for years. She was placing some books on a shelf after the library had closed. She was anxious to get finished and huffed in frustration as she reached for a higher shelf and tripped, almost falling. After a moment, she brushed back a brown curl from her face and returned to her task. Suddenly the whir of the elevator coming up from the first floor startled her and she dropped a book. Aggravated that a fellow employee evidently left the door open, she stopped what she was doing and went to the elevator to inform the passengers that the library was closed. She stood there and prepared her best librarian smile, but when the doors opened the elevator was empty. She felt a cold draft emanating from the open doors and slowly stepped away. She left for the night — taking the stairs to the first floor exit.

Other stories revolve around the students from the nearby colleges who work at the library as interns. One female intern ventured into the periodical storage room to retrieve a manuscript, and as she was searching for it, she suddenly felt a cool draft on the back of her neck and a faint whisper in her ear. She ran from the room and refused to ever go back into that part of the building.

One male intern was working in the resource room when he heard the unmistakable sound of books being pulled from the shelves. A cold draft wafted up from the area. It was then that he heard a man's voice. Peering around the corner, he was about to speak when he realized no one was there. He fled the library, never to return.

Curiously, the apparition that is most often seen strongly resembles William Godber Hinson, who was an avid collector of southern literacy. When he died, he left his extensive collection of books, manuscripts, and newspaper clippings to the Charleston Library Society. Mr. Hinson's portrait hangs in the main reading room — most of the time.

Once it was seen to literally jump off the wall. It's interesting to note that ghostly phenomenon seems to be present throughout the library. Perhaps Mr. Hinson roams the building admiring the contents.

THE HUNLEY SUBMARINE

On a cool morning in 1861, George Dixon stood on the deck at the train station in Alabama with the young lady who had captured his heart. He was leaving to join the 21st Alabama Infantry out of Mobile. He stood watching the sunlight pour through her hair and knew he was going to miss her. She smiled as she handed him a gold coin. Minted in 1860, it was still shiny. George was puzzled. The look on his face must have given him away because Queenie began to giggle. George began to giggle with her. As the laughter died down, Queenie explained that the coin was meant to remind him of her and keep him safe. George promised to keep the coin with him always and promised to return safely.

Lt. George Dixon marched with his comrades onto a Tennessee battlefield in Shiloh on April 6, 1862. In his pocket, he carried the $20 gold coin. During the battle, he was shot point blank in the upper left thigh. The gold coin deflected the bullet from a major artery, saving his life—and so began the legend of the gold coin and Lt. Dixon. More than a hundred years after his death, the legend would be proven to be based in reality.

Historic documents show that Lt. Dixon returned to Mobile, Alabama, to recover from the wounds he received during the Battle of Shiloh. It is speculated that during this time Lt. Dixon met William Alexander, one of the builders of the *Hunley* submarine. As the friendship between the men developed and Lt. Dixon recovered, he joined others aboard the *Hunley* for trial runs in Mobile Bay. In 1863, news from Mobile concerning the successful runs of the *Hunley* had reached Charleston and the plan was born to bring the *Hunley* to Charleston to help fight Union ships.

The *Hunley* made the trip by train and arrived in Charleston in August 1863. The plan was considered a failure, however, as initial test missions proved unsuccessful, eventually taking the lives of thirteen men including Horace Hunley, the submarine's namesake.

Located outside the Warren Lasch Conservation Center is a replica of the *Hunley*.

A determined Lt. Dixon convinced General Beauregard to give the submarine another chance. With General Beauregard's blessing, he pulled together a crew of volunteers and began test missions off the coast of Charleston, earning him the title of "Commander" of the *Hunley*.

On February 17, 1864, the Hunley became the world's first combat submarine when, under Lt. Dixon's command, it successfully sank the Housatonic. Although the mission was successful, the *Hunley* never returned to shore — it disappeared into the murky depths of the sea where it remained for more than 130 years.

On May 3, 1995, the *Hunley* was discovered by Ralph Wilbanks, Wes Hall, and Harry Pecorelli of the National Underwater Marine Agency and excavation began in 2001. On May 25, 2001, Commander Lt. Dixon's remains — as well as the legendary gold coin — were discovered on the *Hunley*. The gold coin was in fact dented on one side and had the following inscription:

Shiloh
April 6, 1862
My life preserver
G.E.D.

For three years, the remains of the *Hunley* crewmembers stayed within the *Hunley* at the Warren Lasch Conservation Center, protected by the Honor Guard on 24-hour watch, and it wasn't long before those who stood watch over the *Hunley* and its precious cargo were reporting paranormal activity.

The Spirits

Steve Burt was the coordinator of the Honor Guard up until his death in early September 2003. Bill Sharpe, a local reporter for Charleston's "Live Five News," reported on the paranormal activity at the *Hunley* in 2003:

> "According to Steve Burt, it was not unusual to hear footsteps and a disembodied voice calling 'Mother' on watch. The activity became so prominent that Burt began to refer to the ghost as 'The Adjuster.' It seems the ghostly presence adjusted the straps on the soldier's uniforms at times. Burt also said that 'these spirits flick me on the ear three times and then gently nudge me on the back.' He further explained, 'There was never a sense of foreboding. They give you a calm, caring feeling almost as if they are glad you are there.'"

Sharpe's report also included the experiences of Randy Burbage, who had helped in recovering the remains of the first *Hunley* crew from under and around the Johnson Haygood Stadium. (Four were recovered from under the stadium and one from in front of it.) Burbage reported feeling led to dig in certain areas around the stadium and would register a "strange feeling." He relayed that every time he got "the feeling" another crew member would be found. Like Burt, Burbage felt that the spirits were friendly and meant no harm.

I spoke with Kellen Correia of the "Friends of the Hunley" and she informed me that despite the Honor Guard's reports of paranormal activity, she has never experienced anything in the building herself that was even remotely paranormal.

My husband and I visited the Warren Lasch Conservation Center in December 2007. During our visit, we took several photos and used a digital voice recorder in the hopes of capturing EVPs. While no anomalies were captured in photos, there was a ghostly whisper on the recorder that we could not identify or explain away. Regardless of the EVP, it was a surreal experience just observing Lt. Dixon's gold coin — and the other contents from his pockets — that are on display at the Center.

Laid to Rest

On April 17, 2004, the *Hunley* crew was interred at Magnolia Cemetery. Commander Lt. Dixon, Arnold Becker, Corporal J. F. Carlsen, Frank Collins, Lumpkin Miller, James A. Wicks, and Joseph Ridgaway are finally at rest — or are they?

Several members of the Honor Guard reported experiencing paranormal activity following the funeral at Magnolia Cemetery. Even Bill Sharpe had an interesting experience on the day of the burial of the crewmembers. In a photo, he was astonished to see...a crewmember staring back at him! The ghostly figure disappeared from the photo a short time later.

The remains of the *Hunley* crew are not the only notable interments at Magnolia Cemetery. Since 1849, senators, congressmen, lawyers, and Civil War soldiers — including eighty-four South Carolinians who died in the Battle at Gettysburg — have been laid to rest there. Amidst the notable government heads and American heroes quietly rest the remains of mothers, fathers, and, sadly, children.

Magnolia Cemetery... The final resting place for the crew of the *Hunley* is here.

Chapter Two:
GRAVEYARDS AND CEMETERIES

MAGNOLIA CEMETERY

To visit Magnolia Cemetery, travel approximately two miles north of Charleston on King Street, turn right at Mount Pleasant Street, left onto Meeting Street and right onto Cunnington Avenue. The cemetery entrance is at 70 Cunnington Avenue.

Margaret and Her Doll

On a warm summer day a little girl walked with a young man through the cemetery. As they strolled, she chatted on about everything that little girls talk about — friends, family, and toys. Her favorite doll was clutched in her hands and the ruffles on her skirt made a swishing sound as she walked. She had never worn such a fine dress.

One of very few death masks in the United States can be found at Magnolia Cemetery, adorned by the sweet face of Rosalie Raymond White.

Mamma painstakingly sewed it from fine linens she had bought only a day before. Her hair was brushed back in loose curls that framed her perfect round face. Her bright pink lips pursed when she thought about the boy who teased her on the banks of the Cooper River.

Charles was finished his chores. On the way to grab his fishing pole, little Margaret tugged on his shirt. He didn't like to take her fishing, but today was different. He gave in to her relentless begging and conceded to take his little sister with him. Charles and Margaret arrived at their favorite spot along Cooper River. Charles' friend William was already there.

On this particular day, the fish weren't biting. William was bored. He had taken Blue Bell — Margaret's favorite doll — and was holding her by the feet, dangling her over the water. Charles was nearby wrestling a squirming worm onto a fishing hook; when he heard his sister squeal, he bolted toward his friend.

As William turned to give Margaret back her doll, he tripped on a rock and lost his balance. As he struggled to regain his step, he lost his grip and Blue Bell fell into the water. Margaret dove in after her and quickly disappeared in the rushing current. Hours later her lifeless body was found floating downstream. Clutched in her right hand was her favorite doll.

The spirits of the child and who is believed to be her father, a soldier killed during the Civil War, are often seen at Magnolia Cemetery on bright and warm summer days. When they are approached, the two simply evaporate, as the little girl giggles.

Little Annie

Little Annie Aiken's plot in Magnolia Cemetery is striking. Atop a marble slab lies the figure of a sleeping child. Her parents were Joseph Daniel Aiken and Ellen Daniel Martin. Joseph Aiken was a prominent lawyer in Charleston.

On a crisp fall afternoon, Keith went about taking photos within the cemetery walls. As he approached the area of the Martin family plot, he noticed a little girl playing among the fall leaves. He watched for a moment perusing the cemetery for her parents. When he realized that no one else was near the little girl, he became concerned. He parked and closed the truck door.

Annie Aiken is buried at Magnolia Cemetery... The ghost of a child has been spotted near the little girl's marker.

He caught sight of her running behind a small unusual monument. When she saw him approaching, she stood silently waiting. She was wearing a white lace gown. Small yellow embroidered flowers dotted the lace. She smiled and crouched down behind the monument once more. Keith approached the area where he had seen her last and entered the family plot. Growing more concerned, he spent several minutes looking for her, but then realized that the ornate iron gate in the fence where he had entered was the only exit from the family plot. The child could not have escaped without him seeing her. Chills ran up his spine as he realized he had just seen a ghost.

The small apparition has been seen numerous times throughout the years and always near Little Annie's plot. According to a former cemetery employee, there is speculation among those who have witnessed the child ghost as to whether it is a boy or a girl. It seems that children's fashion in the 1800s was similar, especially for the very young. Regardless of whether the child is male or female, it seems to be at home near Little Annie Aiken's plot.

Annie spent her young life living at the Greek revival home at 20 Charlotte Street with her parents. The family home has now been converted to an inn. Local legend states that tunnels ran underground to the house. Dark stories speculate that the tunnels were used for illegal slave trade after the Civil War. Supposedly, the brick arch from the top of one of the tunnel entrances that was once underground can be seen from the front of the house. For more information, please visit www.charlottestcarriagehouse.com.

CIRCULAR CONGREGATIONAL CHURCH GRAVEYARD

Circular Congregational Church Graveyard is located at 150 Meeting Street. The oldest known slate marker in the United States is in this graveyard. It is not legible and is surrounded now by wood to keep it from deteriorating further. Another interesting note is that in those days when people bought burial plots, they were allowed to plant gardens on the grave. This is where the term "pushing up daisies" comes from. Be sure to check for times when the cemetery and church are open to the public.

Buried Too Soon

Today, we would take some Tylenol and wait it out. But it was 1760 and little Martha Laurens had a fever. Her parents, Henry and Eleanor, did all they could for her and tried to make her as comfortable as possible. A few days later, the tiny one-year-old succumbed to the illness. Her grieving parents bought a coffin and put Martha on display in the formal parlor by an open window so that friends and family could pay their last respects. Imagine their surprise when little Martha sneezed! Dr. Moultrie pronounced her as indeed living and thus the life of Martha Laurens was spared.

In those days, people in Martha's predicament might well find themselves in a coffin, buried in a graveyard or cemetery with a cord wrapped around their wrist. The cord would be attached aboveground to a bell, which would ring if the prematurely interred moved their arm. The person hired (usually by the family) to watch over the bell would then inform the gravediggers, who would promptly dig up and

The oldest known slate marker in the United States.

The Circular Congregation Church and Graveyard

free the poor person from a most horrifying experience. Sometimes, however, the natural state of the body beginning to decay would cause the arm to move and ring the bell. This is where the terms "dead ringer" and "graveyard shift" come from.

Henry, Martha's father, was so mortified about almost burying his beloved daughter that he swore he would never be buried. So, when Henry Laurens took his last breath on December 8, 1792, the good people of Charleston honored his wishes. The body of Henry Laurens was taken down to the river where the bank was high and steep. First, they tried lining his pockets with grass and hay and set him upon a pile of wood. Unfortunately, only his hair and clothes burned. They soaked him in creosote and set him ablaze once again. Unfortunately, his head fell off and rolled down the steep embankment where one lucky Charlestonian retrieved it before it fell into the Cooper River. Eventually, his body did burn and thus the first cremation on American soil took place. Charleston promptly outlawed cremation in the city until 1905.

As a side note, Martha did not attend her father's cremation and referred to his funeral as "the awful ceremony." She was a devoted daughter and simply could not bear the thought of witnessing the burning of her father's body.

According to her memoirs, Martha lived a full life and was said to be an extraordinary child. She could read every book by the time she was three years old, even if it was held upside down. By the time she reached adulthood, she spoke fluent French. Her loving aunt is credited with giving Martha a fine upbringing with love and support after the death of her mother when she was merely eleven. Martha grew to be a beautiful, graceful, and bright woman. She married Dr. David Ramsay and gave birth to eleven children, eight of whom survived. She also seemed to develop a sort of recognizance when it came to the deaths of her family members. Many members of the Ramsay and Laurens families are now interred at the Circular Congregational Church Graveyard.

Many of Charleston's tour companies now visit the graveyard on a nightly basis. On Martha's grave, there normally sits a tabby cat. Feral cats residing in the cemeteries and graveyards are not unusual in Charleston. However, this cat seems to be particularly fond of Martha and anyone who tells her story. It does not express affection though to those who are not near Martha's grave. As ancient Egyptians believed, could this kitty be Martha's companion in the afterlife and yet guarding her body in this plane of existence?

The Interesting Tale of Dr. Savage

The final resting place of the Savage family....

Here lies the bodies of three brothers
Sons of Richard and Mary Savage
Who were interred within ten days
dære to this Stone
John Clifford Savage died
August 31, 1784, aged 10 years, 5 months, 7 days
William Savage
September 8, 1784, aged 3 years, 6 months
Dandridge Richard Savage
September 9, 1784, aged 5 years, 6 months, 6 days
Beneath the surface of the turfed earth
Enwrapt in silence amid the arms of death
Exposed to worms, lies three once charming boys
The Father's comfort and the Mother's joy
These youths at once fair fruit and blossoms bore
Much in possession, expectance no more
Twou'd grieve you tender reader to relate
The hasty strides of unrelenting fate
Dire decree of human art was vain
The power of medicine failed the healing train
But happy youths by death made truly great
Had life been lengthened to it's utmost date
What had they known but sorrow, pain and woe
The curse entailed on Adam's Race below
They're only safe who through death's gates have passed
And reached those joys that evermore will last
Now vain is Man how fluttering are his joys
When what one moment gives, the next destroys
Hope and Despair fill up his round of life
And all his joys are one continual strife

In the 1700s, Dr. Savage was desperately trying to find a cure for smallpox. Unfortunately, he brought the disease home with him and his three young boys fell victim and died within the same week. The boys were interred together in one plot within the graveyard. By the time of his death, Dr. Savage had also lost his wife, whom he had interred with their sons.

Dr. Savage, like Henry Laurens, had a fear of premature burial. Near the time of his death, a lot of Charlestonians were diagnosed with tuberculosis and were prescribed a morphine-laced cough syrup. As the addiction to morphine took hold, many TB patients would overdose and become unconscious. Because TB is spread through the air, many doctors would pronounce unconscious patients as "dead" because they only briefly wanted to come in contact with the body. They simply didn't stick around long enough to know if the body was still breathing.

Many medical students and grave robbers would dig up a body only to find that it was still living. As was the burial process at the time, the body was usually wrapped in muslin and cotton sheets. This is where our modern day image of the white ghost comes from.

When Dr. Savage passed away, he had an aboveground crypt built on top of the graves of his sons and his wife. He was interred aboveground so that if he, in fact, were mispronounced, he would be able to escape. Sadly, Dr. Savage was indeed dead, but the loving epitaph inscribed on the tomb of his family is worth a visit to the Circular Congregational Church Graveyard *(see previous page)*.

Dr. Savage has been seen on clear moonlit nights sitting quietly atop his grave. He sings and sometimes whistles as he seemingly works away, whittling a stick. When he is approached...he fades and disappears.

THE GHOSTS OF ST. PHILIPS

Near the west entrance gate at St. Philips Graveyard, there is a small sign that reads:

"The only ghost at St. Philips is the Holy Ghost."

It is an appropriate sign. However, there is one thing in common amongst those I've interviewed — they all believe what they've seen. Rightfully so, as it is often difficult to dismiss what we have seen with our own eyes.

I'm sure that when a photographer snapped a quick photo through the closed graveyard fence, inadvertently capturing the apparent apparition of a long deceased woman mourning the loss of her child, the onslaught of attention that the church received must have been a bit overwhelming.

Its History

St. Philips Church has the oldest congregation in Charleston, dating back to 1670. In 1850, the city was growing and asked St. Philips to move the church twenty-five feet so that they could extend Church Street. St. Philips refused. The city officials said, "OK," and simply diverted the extended Church Street around St. Philips. There was only one problem — the graveyard was in the way. City officials moved the markers and headstones, but never moved the bodies that still lay under Church Street today. South Carolina law states that it is legal to build on top of the buried as long as you don't disturb them.

The difference between a graveyard and a cemetery is strictly location. Graveyards are identified as the tract of land next to a church. Cemeteries are generally anywhere else and do not have churches attached to them. In the 1800s, everybody wanted to be buried in the graveyard at St. Philips as opposed to across the street at the cemetery because they believed that the closer you were to the church, the closer you were to God. Because of this, St. Philips had to impose a new rule: If you were a blueblood Charlestonian — or "born, bred, and dead" in Charleston — you could be buried in the graveyard. Otherwise, your remains would be interred in the cemetery across the street.

The steeple tower of St. Philips Church.

At the time of his death, Vice President John C. Calhoun was interred in the graveyard. When the church realized that he had not been born in Charleston, he was moved to the cemetery side. In 1864, the city was afraid that Union troops would take his body and move it up north, so Calhoun's body was re-interred on the graveyard side. Then one day in the early 1900s, a little old lady stood up at a church meeting and politely asked that Mr. Calhoun be vacated from her plot as she was sure she was going to be in need of it soon. Mr. Calhoun was then moved back across the street and re-interred in the cemetery, where he remains today.

Sue Howard Hardy

Sue and her husband desperately wanted to have a baby. After two difficult pregnancies and subsequent miscarriages, she and her husband learned the happy news that they were once again expecting. For nine months Sue prepared for the new arrival. On June 13, 1888 her dreams were shattered as she gave birth to a stillborn baby boy. As was the custom at the time, she was not legally allowed to name or hold the child. The birth was a complicated one and for three days Sue Howard languished. When she passed away on June 16, 1888, her family begged St. Philips to allow her baby to be buried with her. At first the church refused, claiming that the child was full of sin and was not baptized, but eventually gave in. The baby was placed in a sea grass basket and interred with his mother in the graveyard at St. Philips.

On June 13, 1987, the anniversary of the day the infant was stillborn, Harry Reynolds was taking photos for his book Nighttime Charleston. He wanted to take some photos at St. Philips, but the gates were locked. He walked around the side of the cemetery and put the lens of his camera through the iron bars where he snapped off a few frames. When the pictures were developed, he noticed what appeared to be the transparent figure of a woman leaning over her grave. A sea grass basket was clearly seen beside her as she knelt. Could Sue Howard have been mourning her baby ninety-nine years to the day after his death? That is the theory that has been put forth.

I had the opportunity to view the photograph while I was in Charleston. I have developed another theory, however, than the one that has been presented. I have to wonder if the apparition is perhaps instead one of Sue Howard's relatives tending the garden atop her grave. Sea grass baskets are used for just about every chore imaginable in Charleston. Upon viewing the photo, I realized that the sea grass basket that manifested seems to be taller rather than oblong. I also thought that it made more sense historically speaking had the baby been interred in a small sea grass coffin. I also wondered why Sue Howard would be seen kneeling at her own grave in that exact way with the baby's basket sitting beside her. It just made more sense to me that she would have been cradling the baby or at least looking at it.

Many visitors to the graveyard have reported sensations as they near Sue Howard's grave. Pregnant women, in particular, seem to be the focus of some ghostly attention. There have been reports of being pinched, pushed, kicked, pulled, or squeezed. Oddly, visitors who have endured these experiences feel fine once they leave the graveyard grounds.

The Gray Man

The story of a young lady who was attending a dance next to St. Philips and her subsequent death was first mentioned in a book written by Margaret Rhett Martin Charleston Ghosts.

As the story goes, the young lady had a spirited disagreement with her friends concerning the existence of a particular ghost known as the "gray man" in the St. Philips graveyard. On a dare, she promised to enter the cemetery at night and alone—and to leave something behind to prove to her friends that she had been there.

The young lady's name was "Sallie." She was described as being very kind and beautiful. On the night of the dare she was wearing a flowing ball gown and a rose in her hair. Sallie accidentally pinned herself to the ground when she plunged a cane deep into the dirt, catching her dress. Sallie thought that the gray man had captured her and subsequently died from a heart attack.

The ghostly gray man has been seen by many visitors to Charleston and locals alike even to this day. Legend states that

Grave markers inside St. Philips graveyard... A gray apparition has been spotted here.

anyone unfortunate enough to see the gray man will die shortly afterward. However, that doesn't always seem to be the case.

Cindy was tired. She had left her home in Florida and decided to drive up the coastline until she was too tired to continue. After checking into a nearby hotel, she found herself walking down the street in historic downtown Charleston. She hadn't taken a vacation in years. The argument with her ex-fiancé had inspired her to take a few days off to clear her head. As she walked, breathing in the cool night air, she started to relax.

Her stroll led her down Church Street and eventually she found herself standing before St. Philips Church. The full moon moved from behind a cloud and the instant effect of moonlight illuminating the church and subsequent graveyard seemed like a sign to Cindy. All was right with the world and all would be well. Just as she was about to turn and head back to her hotel room, she caught a glimpse of something moving behind the graveyard wall. She stopped and turned, scanning the moonlit landscape. At first, she thought a live person was wandering in the graveyard. Remembering that the gates were locked, she squinted her eyes to take a closer look. There in the graveyard she saw the gray outline of a man. He seemed to be waving in her direction.

The following day Cindy was surprised when her ex-fiancé showed up at the hotel and, proclaiming his love for her, asked forgiveness for such a silly argument. She returned to Florida and they were married before Christmas. They remain a happily married couple today.

Chapter Three:

OLD PLANTATION HAUNTS

BOONE HALL PLANTATION

Tours to the public began in 1956. For more information, please visit their website at www.boonehallplantation.com.

Spirited Activity

Jim, the former general manager at Boone Hall, locked up the plantation house and retired to his apartment upstairs. In the wee hours of the morning, he heard what sounded like voices coming from the downstairs parlor. Thinking someone had come into the

Boone Hall Plantation, circa 1811.

house, he made his way downstairs. No one was there. Later, as the morning light splashed through the windows of the old plantation house, Jim woke and made his way down the stairs. Every door stood open...yet nothing was missing and nothing was touched.

The head tour guide was alone in the house awaiting the next tour when she heard the unmistakable sound of the whoosh of a hoop skirt and footsteps. Thinking another guide had come in, she turned to greet them. The room was empty. She grabbed her elbows as a chill came over her and paused for a moment before going on to say that many times she will hear voices when no one else is in the house. She could only describe them as "conversations from the past" because the language, although English, was different than the way people speak to each other today.

Another tour guide was leading a group through the outside grounds near the slave cabins when one of the women in the group asked if she could share something. She told the story of how on her last visit she saw a lady wearing a long white gown in the plantation garden. She and her husband were touring the

The front gardens at Boone Hall Plantation... The apparition of a woman has been seen strolling here.

grounds when they paused along the avenue just inside the gate on the walkway going up to the main house. To the left were the gardens and, out of the corner of her eye, she saw the figure of a woman standing near the center of the garden. She was dressed in a white flowing gown and was translucent. The tourist stopped and pointed in the direction of the apparition just as the lady in white disappeared before her eyes.

Several visitors to Boone Hall have born witness to another eerie event. A soldier bent over another man in a field on the plantation appears to be attempting to remove a bullet from the injured man. Their bodies are transparent and echoing screams of agony can be heard.

Possibly the most reported apparition seen at Boone Hall Plantation is what is believed to be a brick-builder. Making the bricks on the plantation was hard labor. Slaves worked long hours each day and fired the handmade bricks in a kiln. The apparition is seen near the place where the old kiln used to be, his hands moving rapidly as though he's stoking the fire.

I interviewed the tour manager at Boone Hall Plantation. According to her, older legends persist at Boone Hall. One such legend states that a beheaded slave comes back every seven years to look for buried Civil War treasure. The tour manager stated this would be impossible because the Horlbeck family owned the plantation during the Civil War era and were making bricks and tile. She believes there would be no treasure to find.

History of Boone Hall

Boone Hall Plantation began in 1681. Major John Boone was aboard one of the first ships to bring settlers to Charleston. South Carolina had been given to Lord's Proprietors of which John Boone was a deputy in 1670. After his marriage, John Boone built the original plantation house.

In 1743, Major John Boone's son planted carefully spaced live oak trees and began the first cash crop of indigo and then cotton. Today, the grand entrance to the plantation is lined with a beautiful canopy of oak trees that stretches from both sides of the avenue. The plantation thrived until 1811 when it was sold to

A slave cabin built from damaged bricks manufactured at Boone Hall Plantation.

The interior view of a slave cabin on Boone Hall Plantation.

62   Old Plantation Haunts

Thomas Bardell. He sold it six years later to the Horlbeck family and they began manufacturing brick and tile on the plantation. The Horlbecks built the house that now stands on the plantation, as well as the slave quarters; the latter was made of damaged bricks produced on the grounds. It's reported that the Boone family was very favorable towards their slaves. The plantation was noted as a "good" place to live and work.

In the early 1920s, the plantation was sold to a Russian prince. The prince reportedly began an affair with one of the Gullah women who lived on the property. She taught him "black magic," according to the tour guides. When he and his wife divorced in the 1940s, the plantation was sold to the McRae family and they still own it today.

Could one of the Horlbecks have watched from the garden as her husband left for war? Could the Russian prince have developed a close relationship with one of the Gullah women who lived on the property? Could apparitions still roam the corridors? Boone Hall Plantation is still keeping some of its secrets.

CONGAREE PLANTATION/ FORT MOTTE

In 1758, Rebecca Brewton and Jacob Motte were married. The couple was the epitome of Charleston aristocracy of the time. They enjoyed a rich and fulfilling life, reared five children, and owned a plantation outside Charleston on the banks of the Congaree River. The couple lived quietly, spending most of their time at the Charleston townhouse...until the outbreak of the Revolutionary War.

By 1776, when the war came to Charleston, Jacob had become very ill. Rebecca was a patriot and decided that since her husband was physically unable and she had no sons (their only infant son had died shortly after birth), she would do her best to do what she could for her country. She sent word that the plantation and able-bodied men were at the disposal of the American soldiers to help with building fortifications and manual labor. Those efforts paid off as the British were held at bay until 1780.

A War Heroine

Sir Henry Clinton is credited for the successful overtaking of Charleston. The Motte family home was commandeered and became the headquarters for Clinton and his staff. Documentation shows that the Motte family was forced to live in one room while Clinton and his staff lived in luxury throughout the rest of the home. Rebecca Motte developed an uneasy relationship with the invaders and was said to often preside over the dinner table. She strictly forbade her daughters from appearing before the men and they were, therefore, imprisoned in the small room with their ailing father. Unfortunately, she lost her husband on a cold January day in 1781.

Rebecca Motte secured permission to leave Charleston and returned to her beloved plantation shortly after her husband's death. Unfortunately it wasn't long before the British decided to build a military station on the estate. The plantation became known as Fort Motte. The girls were once again forced to live in one room until the invaders banished them altogether to a small farmhouse on the premises. There, the women found ingenious ways to hide family heirlooms in the unfinished walls, small pieces at a time. The soldiers never discovered the loot.

When Col. Henry Lee arrived at Fort Motte, there was great discussion about the best way in which to reclaim the plantation. Rebecca Motte had an idea. According to legend, she presented to Col. Lee a quiver of arrows that were reputed to set aflame any wood that they struck. Fearing that more British reinforcements would arrive, Col. Lee gave the order and three of the arrows were launched. Although all three met their mark, only the one that landed on the shingles set the plantation home ablaze. The British were unable to extinguish the fire and ultimately surrendered. Col. Lee and his troops extinguished the flame and Rebecca Motte was revered as a hero. When praised over her role in the siege, she would say, "Too much has been made of a thing that any American woman would have done." After the end of the war, Ms. Motte returned to the townhouse in Charleston where she lived until her death in 1815. Rebecca Motte was interred in St. Philips Graveyard.

The Spirits

On a crisp winter evening, Jeanette and Carol McEver were walking along King Street. The sisters had come to Charleston from Boston for the funeral of a dear family friend. As happens quite a bit in Charleston, the two were stopping here and there along the street and commenting on the various architectural accents. As they approached an unassuming brick townhouse, the pair stopped and chatted. The conversation turned to the family friend who lost her life to a debilitating disease and was house-bound for several years. As Jeanette was looking at the architecture, she was the first to see a young woman peering out of a window. The girl seemed sad and had a longing look on her face. Her hair was pulled up and the sisters thought that she must be a re-enactor based on her clothing. Jeanette waved to the girl, who vanished. After relaying the story to other Charleston friends, the girls were surprised to learn the history of the house.

About thirty-five miles from Charleston, there is a bridge that crosses onto an old country road that leads to the site of the old Motte House Plantation. The location was off Syne Road and in the vicinity of Wise Road and Moye Lane. In 2004, a group of students from the University of South Carolina began an archeological dig on the property. While retrieving musket balls and canister rounds, one student had an unearthly experience.

Near what is believed to be the foundation of the home, the student was working to dislodge an artifact when he heard a female voice say "stop." Thinking that one of his colleagues was teasing him, he turned to talk to her. Standing about four feet behind him was not a colleague, but instead who he can only describe as Rebecca Motte. He had seen some of the historic portraits of Mrs. Motte and recognized her almost instantly. She was wearing a long dress with small detailed lace around the collar and sleeves. He asked her if she really wanted him to stop and the apparition answered, "No, be careful. They'll see you." As he stood to continue the conversation, she took a step forward and disappeared. When I asked the student if anything in particular stood out to him, he only said she had piercing blue eyes.

ANGEL OAK PLANTATION

Like those before them, Jacob and Sarah Waight stood on the deck of the ship and watched in awe as they entered the Charles Towne Harbor at what was then called "Oyster Point." A long and nail-biting journey from England aboard the Edista had brought them to this great new land where they had been granted 12,000 acres on what would become John's Island by Lord Anthony Ashley Cooper for the purpose of establishing a Quaker town. Along with hopeful passengers, the ship carried a cargo of furniture, a prized collection of quilted skirts, and other linens and materials.

Sarah and Jacob remained on the land until Sarah's death in 1717. In her last will and testament, she left the land — including a massive oak tree — to her nephew, Abraham Waight. The great tree stayed in the Waight family for four generations before becoming part of a wedding gift to Justus Angel and his wife, Martha Waight Tucker Angel.

Justus Angel came to Charleston from the island of Santa Cruz in Bermuda. He took an oath of allegiance on June 10, 1801, and began work as a shopkeeper living at various addresses in

The legendary Angel Oak Tree... It's the oldest living tree east of the Rockies.

downtown Charleston. He and his wife, Martha, were married November 23, 1810 and began having social events under the massive oak tree soon after their wedding, enjoying family gatherings with friends.

Tulu and "Man"

An elderly black woman sat in a chair on the porch outside her residence in a less traveled part of Charleston. She was referred to me by a friend and was willing to be interviewed about some of the Gullah legends that persist even to this day. As the sun set, casting orange hues across her face, she leaned back and began to speak.

She told a story of massive birds making their homes in the great oak tree on St. John's Island. The huge nests were high in the branches. "In the old days, the birds enjoyed feasting on those that were hanged — wayward slaves from a nearby plantation." The slave spirits are said to haunt the old oak and large birds are still making their homes in the tree. She went on to say that there are "many burials beneath the tree." Slaves were not the only burials there. The ancient tree was once a gathering place for Native Americans who lived on the island and many Native American burials are reported to be on the grounds. The Native Americans who once lived on the land contributed to the health of the tree and its massive growth, and it is believed that their spirits still stand guard. This could be one reason why nighttime visitors experience a sense of foreboding. As the conversation continued and we found an easy acquaintance with each other, she told me a fascinating story.

"Tulu was a beautiful baby. Her brown skin and wavy hair were intriguing to her Master. But what he found most appealing were her beautiful blue eyes. He persuaded his wife to move the infant and her mother into the plantation home so that they could work as house servants. As Tulu grew, the Master's love for her grew. He never raised his voice to her and over time found himself attempting to appease her every wish.

Because it was the law that slave owners could not own the soul of their slaves, only their bodies, my great-great-grandmother was allowed to leave the plantation with her family on Sundays to attend Church. It was there that (Tula) met her beloved. She fell in love when she was but sixteen years old. In those days it was difficult for a slave to marry, let alone outside your own plantation as this would present a multitude of problems. Most marriages weren't recognized and any children born of the union also became the property of the slave owner.

To further complicate matters, Tulu's owner and the owner of the man she was in love with were rivals. My family did not remember his name and my Mamma always called him 'the man.' She would say it with a very serious look in her eyes and I always knew that it meant something important, although I was too young to understand exactly what. Anyway, Tulu and the Man would meet as often as they could. It was hard on them. They had to rely on family and friends to cover for them at the plantation for the short minutes that they could steal together. They would meet at the big oak tree near the plantation where Tulu lived. They call that tree 'Angel Oak.'

One night Tulu and Man met at the old oak tree. He had proposed to her only two days before and the excited couple couldn't wait to make wedding plans. As they talked, time ticked away and soon Tulu was being missed at the plantation. When her Master went looking for her, he was full of concern that something terrible had happened. He had never missed her at the plantation in the evening before and couldn't imagine where she might be. After searching the island extensively, he decided to ride his horse out to the great oak tree to pray. There, his heart was broken.

He discovered Tulu and her beloved under the limbs of the massive oak caught in a loving embrace. Her Master became insane with jealousy and Tulu's beloved was immediately hanged from a low limb. Tulu was beaten before the Master brought her back to the plantation. From that day forward, he treated her with disdain. Brokenhearted, on a dark night a few weeks later Tulu returned to the tree where she used a knife to slice her arms and bled to death."

The Spirits of Angel Oak

Although many apparitions have been seen around the tree and several people have claimed to have spiritual experiences under the massive branches, I never expected to have my own spiritual experience on my visit to Angel Oak. When I arrived with friends in tow, there was an instant aura of peace. The tree was truly magnificent and breathtaking. We paused in silence for a long while under the branches, walking back and forth.

Now, I am a city girl at heart, but I do live in the outskirts of Atlanta in a more rural part of the city. There are horse and chicken farms within five miles of my home. In my backyard stands my own old oak tree. (I had a landscaper once tell me it was more than 300-years-old.) I am grateful that our homebuilder left it. I have also hiked up several hills to stand beneath beautiful waterfalls and I enjoy camping. So, I'm no stranger to the woods or how various plants can look in photographs. But I was truly stunned at what happened at Angel Oak and the incredible photo that I captured during my visit.

It was a hot summer day and yet standing beneath the shade of the branches, even the humidity seemed to decrease. I stood in awe. The sunlight was peeking through the clouds behind the tree, giving it an eerie glow. As I stood there, I began to hear a woman's voice. She was calling out and I could hear her, albeit faintly. I looked around and heard the voice again — soft and low, giggling in sheer delight. I noticed a woman with two small children coming into the area from the visitor's center. Believing the voice must have belonged to the woman, I thought nothing more of it...until I came home and downloaded my photos to my computer.

I took several pictures of the tree from several angles. As I was perusing them I paused when something about one of the photos seemed a little "off." After a moment, I realized that there was something odd about the woman standing near a massive branch towards the back of the tree. I put the photo into my software and zoomed in on the area. What I saw was perplexing. The woman was not transparent, but cast an eerily translucent glow. She was not floating. She was not there at the time the photo was taken. Indeed, she seemed to be from an earlier time period. She seemed to wearing a long gown with her hands reaching behind her back.

At first, I thought she was a figment of my imagination — the misinterpreted image of a sunlit tree trunk. (Our brains will play all kinds of tricks on us as our eyes focus.) But as I looked closely I realized that other photos of the same area indicated no tree where she seemed to be standing. More than that; her arms, her gown, and her hair could clearly be seen.

I took the photo to my local Wolf Camera store along with the other photos of the area. There, I asked the staff to debunk the photo and to send it to whoever could help me ascertain what it might be. All the results from these professional photo experts came back the same. They could not identify what the anomaly was and considered it to be a true apparition.

On closer examination, some who have seen the original photo can make out a man standing in front of the woman. He is facing her and seems to be wearing 1940s clothing. Both figures are in profile.

In my career, I have seen few photos that I believe are actual paranormal anomalies. I have had a couple of things show up in photos I have taken, but nothing compares to this incredible photo taken under the Angel Oak tree. Is she a lost spirit looking for her loved ones? Could she be an ethereal being drawn to the tree? Or maybe somehow on that particular day a window in time was opened, even if only for a second.

The tree (and subsequent park) is now owned by the City of Charleston. There is no admission fee to visit. For more information, please visit www.angeloaktree.org or give them a call at (803) 559-3496.

Untouched photo of an apparition (toward the back right) under Angel Oak Tree. Apparition shown in inset.

Chapter Four:
HAUNTED EATERIES

BOCCI'S ITALIAN RESTAURANT
58 Church Street
www.boccis.com

Spirits Abound

Kelly sat at her desk in her third floor office at Bocci's Italian Restaurant. As she worked, she heard someone knock on the door. Thinking a staff member had come up to speak with her, she called out, "Come in!" When no one entered the office, she walked around

Bocci's Italian Restaurant, circa 1867.

her desk and opened the door. The corridor was empty. Sure that some one was playing a joke on her, she searched all the third floor offices. Kelly was the only staff member on the third floor. She returned to her desk a bit shaken.

The third floor offices seem to be a mecca for all sorts of paranormal activity. Several staff members have heard disembodied voices whispering around dark corners. The staff break room has been host to the dead as well as the living. The apparitions of children have also been seen on the third floor. However, there isn't really an area of Bocci's that is safe from the spiritual realm.

On a cool September night, as one of the staff was cleaning up on the second floor, he saw what he believed to be the kitchen manager crouched down by a wall. "Andy?" he called out. "What are you doing?" There was no reply. As he moved closer, he realized that the figure was a man with dark hair and deep black eyes crouching down by the wall near the door. Moving closer, he saw that the man was...completely transparent.

Bocci's was built in 1867 by the Molony family. The building housed Charleston's first Irish Pub downstairs and the family lived upstairs. Business continued as usual during Prohibition when the bar was secretly moved to the back of the building and operated as a speakeasy. The family opened a grocery store in front of the building. Although the building switched hands several times, the original structure remains intact. In fact, if you look closely at the brick side from Cumberland Street, you can still see the original "Jax Beer" sign.

TOMMY CONDON'S IRISH PUB

Tommy Condon's is right next door to Bocci's Italian Restaurant. I visited the restaurant thinking that whatever is causing the friendly phenomenon at Bocci's probably makes its way to Tommy Condon's as well. I was wrong.

Bothersome Spirits

Victoria was a little upset. She wasn't supposed to be assigned to the "bad section," but another server called out sick and things were switched around at the last minute. Being assigned to the tables with the least tips was annoying, but there was also a constant uneasiness in the room that made the hair on the back of her neck stand on end. She felt like she was being watched too, especially in the server station.

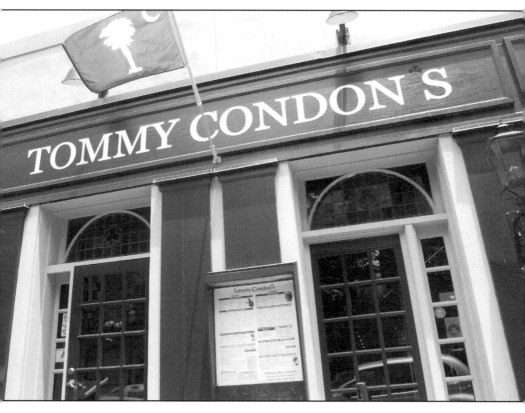

Tommy Condon's Irish Pub was used as a candy warehouse in the early 1900s.

After a long day and not as many tips as she had hoped, Victoria was cleaning up. An empty coffee cup was on one of the tables and as she moved about getting things ready for the next day she spotted it and made a mental note to put the cup away and clean the table. Victoria returned to the service station and, soon after, heard a loud bang! As she ran out to see what had happened, she saw it. The coffee cup had tipped over with such force that it knocked over the sugar holder and broke into pieces. Victoria left immediately and didn't return until the following morning, refusing to work the area.

Other stories are centered on the ladies restroom. The toilet paper in the handicap-equipped stall spins out of control. A haggard old lady is sometimes spotted in the mirror...only to disappear. Unseen hands open and close the baby changing station and then there is the issue of the stall doors.

Janice was in the restroom. She and her husband are regulars at Tommy Condon's. She had heard the stories from other customers and staff alike, but she hadn't really experienced anything other than goose bumps now and then. Janice had always been paranoid about locking the stall door, even when she was a little girl. As she went about attending to nature's call, the stall door suddenly swung open! Knowing she had locked and closed it, Janice left the ladies room more than a little shaken.

A staff member who worked for years at Tommy Condon's in the kitchen before his death has been seen on many occasions. The apparition is usually seen in the back near a storage area, apparently going about his daily routine. On some nights he makes his presence known in other ways. Stove burners will turn themselves off and on, which is sometimes a frightening thought for those who work in the kitchen. But perhaps the most intriguing story involves the spirit of a child.

In the early 1900s, the building where Tommy Condon's now stands was a candy warehouse. There is an old loading track laid within the restaurant that curves around the bar. One night at closing, Sharon was ready to go home. She walked toward the door, pausing to retrieve her car keys out of her purse. She heard the sound of a child singing and turned around to see whose child it was. There, standing near the bar was a little girl approximately five years old. She was wearing a pink dress with ruffles and her hair was pulled up in pigtails. At first she seemed completely normal. But within a second or so, Sharon realized that the little girl was transparent. Mesmerized, she continued to stare and soon heard the sound of metal wheels on a track. As the sound grew louder, Sharon began to panic. She watched in horror as the ghostly cart hurried along the track and passed through the little girl. Sharon covered her eyes and screamed. As the remaining staff came running, she opened her eyes only to discover that the little girl had disappeared. Without saying a word, she turned and left, but after that experience, Sharon never returned to Tommy Condon's to work.

Whatever draws you to Tommy Condon's, be it a fantastic menu or the ambience, one thing is for sure...not all the spirits are listed on the menu. For more information, visit their website at www. tommycondons.com or call 843-577-3818.

MAD RIVER GRILLE

32 North Market Street
www.madrivercharleston.com

Spirited Happenings

When Mad River Bar & Grille first opened its doors, some of the staff used to spend the night in the building instead of driving home to Summerville. They thought sleeping in sleeping bags on the floor would give them an opportunity to rest after a long day before beginning work again in the early morning hours. They couldn't have been more wrong.

The staff settled into their sleeping bags, cracking jokes and generally in a good mood, but exhausted. Soon, they fell into a deep slumber. In the wee hours of the morning, they were awakened by the sound of bottles breaking on the floor. At first glance, they thought that maybe the shelf the bottles were resting on was slanted or broken. Neither was the case. The staff watched in horror as a bottle shook and then lifted off the shelf and fell to the floor in front of it. The bottles continued to fly off the shelves for several weeks. The staff's "slumber parties" at Mad River were shortlived.

On Thanksgiving day in 2006, the general manager came in to open the restaurant for the evening around 7:30 p.m. The restaurant would open for business at 9 p.m. for an evening of celebration. The manager and assistant manager decided to share a meal before beginning the night's festivities. They brought in some steaks, and as the manager cooked them on the grill, his assistant set up the

Mad River Bar & Grille was once a seamen's chapel, circa 1815.

bar for the evening. After dinner, the manager was cleaning up and took the plates into the kitchen. There, he noticed that the heat lamps were turned on. Annoyed at what he thought was a waste of energy, he returned to the dining room and asked his assistant if he turned on the lamps. He had not, and in fact he hadn't even been in the kitchen.

It's not unusual for whatever resides at the Mad River to wreak havoc with the electrical system. Lights come on and turn off by themselves, as well as the television and audio system. However, perhaps the strangest incident involved the General Manager's office equipment.

Sean came in one morning to meet with an engineer about installing some new computer equipment in his office. He turned the key and stepped inside. He was immediately alarmed. The PC at his desk was turned on its side along with the electric calculator. The power strip had been manually switched off. Knowing that there was only one other person who had a key to his office, he immediately called and questioned his assistant, but he knew nothing of the electrical mishaps.

Beautiful stained glass windows at the Mad River Bar & Grille *(see History next page)*.

The Restaurant's History

In 1745, the Pickney family of Charleston purchased the property where Mad River Grille now stands, but by 1815, they had donated the property so that a non-denominational chapel could be built for visiting sailors to have a place to worship regardless of their faith. Funds to erect the chapel were provided by the Charleston Port Society and the Episcopal Church. In 1916, Bishop Guercy consecrated the Episcopal Church of the Redeemer, but by 1964, the church was no longer needed and was officially deconsecrated. The religious symbols were removed when the building became a fine dining restaurant in 1967.

Today, Mad River Grille is housed within the walls that were once a sanctuary and where prayers of thanksgiving were whispered from those who were safe from the raging seas. Although the original main chapel was in another part of the building, the beauty of the architecture and stained glass that remains adds to the mystique and the paranormal activity that occurs there.

POOGAN'S PORCH

72 Queen Street
www.poogansporch.com

Home Spirit Home

On a warm July night in 2006, Lisa peered from her hotel window and noticed someone in the restaurant across the street. She watched as what appeared to be an elderly woman cross back and forth in front of the upstairs window. The woman kept pacing, only stopping to peer out the window. Thinking she was confused and had wandered into the building, Lisa notified the front desk. They, in turn, called the local police. When the police arrived, they found the restaurant was locked and closed. There were no signs of a break-in and no one was in the building.

The following day Lisa and her daughter had lunch at the restaurant. During the meal, Lisa mentioned the nighttime visitor

Poogan's Porch... Numerous paranormal experiences have been reported here. The restaurant was first built as a private residence in 1888.

to the server. Moments later, she and her daughter were shown a photo of Zoe St. Amand, a previous resident of the home. Lisa positively identified the nighttime visitor as Zoe. She was shocked to learn that Zoe had died in 1954; however, many visitors to the restaurant have seen her….

One member of the staff came in on a cool morning and began his day with a cup of coffee. He walked up the stairs to begin prep work for the day and remembered that he had forgotten to unlock the back door. He set down the coffee cup at the head of the stairs and went back down to unlock the back door. When he returned, his coffee was nowhere in sight. Thinking he was becoming absent minded, he went back down the stairs and made a second cup of coffee. As he climbed the staircase yet again, he noticed the original coffee cup exactly where he left it. The only difference was that there was red lipstick on the rim. It scared him enough that he went outside and waited for other staff members to arrive.

On another occasion, a staff member was upstairs and saw a woman go into the restroom. Knowing no one else should be in the building, he became concerned. He walked to the restroom and called out. When no one answered, he pushed on the restroom door, but it was met with resistance as if someone was behind the door, holding it. As the door gave way, he saw the reflection of a woman in the restroom mirror. She was wearing a white flannel dress with lace on the collar and sleeves. She was also wearing a brim hat with a ribbon around it. As the door opened, he felt a cool breeze as though someone was walking past him.

If one thing was absolutely clear on my first visit to Poogan's Porch, it was the positive energy exuding from the staff. It's clear that they are much more than coworkers. There is an obvious caring for each other — and a deep pride in the restaurant. Perhaps the positive energy is also due to the caring of the invisible residents that still reside there.

It's A Dog's Life

Poogan's Porch was named for the love of a sweet dog named Poogan that lived near the restaurant and became a frequent visitor during renovations. When the restaurant opened, Poogan

The grave of the beloved "Poogan"... The pet has been sensed — *and seen* — throughout the restaurant.

was on the porch to greet the first customers. Poogan became known throughout Charleston and customers were delighted to visit on the porch with the sweet dog. Poogan died in 1979. The beloved pet was buried in the front yard, where he still rests today. Many visitors who dine on the porch report feeling a dog brushing by their legs and sometimes licking their hands.

One of the strangest stories was that of the maintenance man. He came in one day to sweep and mop the hardwood floors. Moments after entering the downstairs dining room, he approached the daytime chef and asked him if the owner had been in that day. When the chef replied that the owner had not been in for several days, the maintenance man insisted that the chef follow him to the dining room. There on the floor was a fresh pile of dog poop. (The owner had a small dog.)

A Safe Call

Isaac yelled at his alarm clock as he woke up late on Thanksgiving morning and hurried to hail a taxi to work at Poogan's Porch. An hour later he found himself muttering under his breath as he entered the cab, his thoughts turning to the broth that was left on the stove to simmer the night before. There was a special menu planned for the afternoon that would require patience and time...both of which Isaac was running out of.

As the taxi closed in on Queen Street, Isaac noticed the fire engine and a tower of smoke. From his vantage point, it appeared that the fire was elsewhere, behind the restaurant. Isaac became impatient with the traffic and left the taxi, walking the short distance to the restaurant. As he drew closer, he realized the smoke was rising from the back of the restaurant, near the kitchen. Not wanting to interfere, Isaac stood on the sidewalk waiting for the firemen to finish. It wasn't until he heard the panicked screams of his boss that he realized she thought he was inside. He hurried across the street and boss and employee embraced in the sheer joy of knowing each other were safe.

Isaac felt lucky that day, but as the hours wore on and he returned home, he thought it was much more than a coincidence that kept him from arriving at work on time. He walked into his bedroom and picked up his alarm clock. To his surprise, the clock was set to the appropriate time, yet somehow didn't go off until exactly an hour later. Isaac has worked at Poogan's since the day they opened in 1976. He calls the restaurant "home." Ghosts have been known to affect electronic equipment and time seems to have no meaning. Perhaps Zoe was instrumental in keeping Isaac safe on that Thanksgiving Day.

Chapter Five:

HOTEL GHOSTS

MILLS HOUSE HOTEL

When the Mill House was built in 1851, it was located adjacent to an old Quaker Cemetery dating back to the early 1700s. In 1973, after years of renovations, the hotel was torn down to its foundation and rebuilt. The contractors used the original Mill House architectural plans to rebuild and restore the hotel to its former glory. Several of the original architectural features were preserved and used in the restoration including the ironwork on the Queen Street balconies. Visit them online at www.millshouse.com or call them at 843-577-2400.

Lost Little Girl

Sharon pulled into the parking garage near the Mills House Hotel. She pulled down the visor and checked her hair in the mirror. It was a warm breezy day and she had driven into Charleston with the windows down. As she primped, she saw in the reflection what appeared to be a very young girl standing about fifteen feet behind her car. The little girl was wearing a plain brown dress and black boots. The child stood, shifting her feet, and seemed to be watching Sharon primp. Sharon noticed that the little girl was still there as she returned her visor to its original position and opened her car door. She wondered where the child's mother was and why she was left alone in the parking garage. As Sharon walked toward her, the little girl turned, walked through a cement wall, and disappeared.

Mills House Hotel... Several different ghosts reportedly inhabit this hotel.

Attempting Contact

On the fifth floor of the hotel, in room 509, Margaret was spending a long weekend in Charleston with her sister, Liz. As they returned to the hotel after an evening of sightseeing, they walked along a corridor on the way to their room. As they walked, Margaret was clicking off various photos with her camera. The next day, when the sisters were reviewing the pictures, the mysterious figure of a man could be seen in the corridor outside their room. He was transparent and wearing what appeared to be a top hat.

The women decided to attempt to communicate with whatever spirits might be residing in their room. As the sun was setting, they lit candles and stood before a mirror. Margaret clicked off more photos as the women attempted to speak to their ghostly visitor. In a moment of silence, a loud knocking sound came from the door. Liz ran to open the door only to find no one standing in the corridor. The two women decided to leave for a while and blew out the candles before taking in some of the warm night air. When they returned to the room an hour later, the candles were relit. The flames danced and flickered as the ladies entered the room. As Liz went to blow the candles out, she noticed the temperature seemed to drop as she moved closer to the candles.

A Messenger from Heaven

Cindy and Dave were staying on the second floor of the hotel. They came to Charleston after the death of their son, Zachary. Zach was born with big blue eyes and a head full of dark curly locks that Cindy casually twirled around her finger. Unfortunately Zachary was also born with a heart defect and passed away quietly in his mother's arms when he was only nine-days-old. Dave thought that a week in Charleston would help provide a distraction for his wife although he knew that nothing would take away the pain.

After spending a couple days sight-seeing in the city, Dave suggested that they spend some time at the beach. Later that night, after enjoying an exquisite dinner across the street at

Poogan's Porch, the two were watching TV in their room. As Cindy snuggled down, surrounded by the comforting arms of her husband, she drifted off into a sound sleep. Sometime around 2 a.m., Cindy woke to the sound of a child's laughter. As she thought about what might have been, tears welled up in her eyes. Suddenly, the child began to sing. A strange feeling of warmth washed over her. She gently shook Dave. As the two cuddled, wrapped in each other's arms, they listened intently as a small child sang and laughed. When the sounds began to drift closer, the two sat up in bed. From the corner of her eye, Cindy saw the shadowy figure of small child floating toward her from the balcony. She noticed that the child had dark curly hair and big blue eyes. Dave sat motionless as he watched the child extend his little hand toward Cindy before disappearing completely.

The next morning, the couple approached the front desk inquiring about the child. There were no children under twelve at the hotel that night. The couple knew that the happy, singing toddler was their "messenger from heaven," sent to let them know that little Zachary was in good hands. Cindy and Dave say that the sorrow they felt when they lost their son has never fully returned. The couple found peace on the second floor at the Mills House Hotel in Charleston.

BATTERY CARRIAGE HOUSE INN

The original Battery Carriage House Inn was built in 1843 by Samuel Stevens. By 1859, the home was sold to John F. Blalock. By 1870, the home had changed hands again and was sold to Colonel Lathers, who had the home remodeled by famous Charleston architect John Henry Devereaux. In 1874, the home was sold to Andrew Simonds, the great-great-grandfather of Drayton Hastie, the current owner. For more information, visit their website at www.batterycarriagehouseinn.com.

The Battery Carriage House Inn, circa 1843. Once used as a Civil War artillery installation, there have been many sightings of Confederate apparitions here.

Spectrophilia

Spectrophilia is defined as the sexual attraction of ghosts. The following story was told to me during an interview with a woman who was once a guest at the Battery Carriage House Inn.

Angela was visiting Charleston with her husband. They chose the Battery Carriage House Inn for a romantic weekend getaway. After a long day of strolling around the historic district and taking in all that Charleston had to offer, the couple retired to their room. Although her husband fell asleep almost immediately, Angela lay still and quiet, reminiscing about the day. She was just starting to drift off when she suddenly had the feeling of being watched. From the corner of her right eye she saw a wispy shape. She turned and saw a man floating near the ceiling. He was transparent and, although she couldn't make out his features very well, she knew that it was a man.

The "Gentleman Caller" is usually sensed in the upstairs guest rooms, startling visitors.

When the figure disappeared, Angela was relieved and thought that she must have been dreaming. A few moments later, she closed her eyes and fell into a deep sleep. At 2 a.m., she was awakened by the feeling of her husband rubbing her arm. As he embraced her, she smiled and opened her eyes...only to find that her husband was no longer in bed! Instead, she found herself embraced by the figure of a man with no discernible facial features. Angela screamed.

She relayed the event to me with a shudder. Angela said that the ghostly embrace was warm in the beginning. However, the reason she opened her eyes was because she grew concerned when she realized his skin was ice cold. When her husband heard Angela scream, he turned on the lights only to find her standing a few feet away from the bed, shaking. It was hours before Angela could bring herself to settle back down to sleep in her husband's arms.

The "Gentleman Caller" has startled many of the guests at the Battery Carriage House Inn. However, he is not the only spirit that seeks attention. During the Civil War, several deaths occurred in and around the property, but none more heartbreaking as the story of the headless torso.

Civil War Casualty

During the Civil War, the inn was used as an artillery installation. As was the normal procedure of the day, Confederate soldiers exploded the artillery in an effort to keep it from falling into enemy hands.

On a fateful day in February a young Confederate soldier went about the business of following orders before leaving Charleston. His orders consisted of blowing up the remaining artillery. Sadly, he misjudged and didn't move away fast enough. The young soldier was ripped to pieces in the blast, leaving only a headless torso.

On a cool winter night in 1995, Samantha was quietly reading a brochure as her husband showered. From the corner of her eye, she saw movement across the room close to the windows. She turned to see a man standing by her bed. The man had "no face and no other discernible body parts save his stomach and chest." Frightened, she moved toward the restroom to retrieve her husband, when the apparition suddenly disappeared. "He was dressed in what appeared to be a confederate uniform."

When I asked Samantha if she was afraid of the apparition, she said that although she had a general sense of foreboding, she thought it was more due to the fact that the apparition was headless than the thought of actually witnessing a ghost.

THE JOHN RUTLEDGE HOUSE INN

Love...

Mr. Smith and his wife wanted children. They had been trying to conceive for several years to no avail. Realizing that attempting to conceive each month and the impending emotional devastation that followed caused so much pain, the couple gave up.

In the spring of 2001, the couple stayed at the Rutledge Victorian Guest House. They were enjoying a quiet evening in the "Victoria Suite" when Mr. Smith felt a presence sit beside him on the bed. When he turned to look, no one was there. Exactly nine months later, the couple gave birth to a baby girl...they named her "Victoria."

... And Loss

Rutledge was built in 1887 by a wealthy tobacco baron, Mr. Pinkussohn. The home originally was five stories high and had a widow's walk. Legend states that in the 1980s a fire broke out at the inn. Sarah, the daughter of the owner, was trapped and killed. Since then, Sarah's ghost has been seen (and smelled) numerous times in the third floor suite. Sarah seems to have a mischievous personality and enjoys turning lights off and on at the most unexpected times.

George and Linda stayed at the inn in 2002. They had just returned from a stroll when they opened the door to the Sarah Suite. The smell of smoke wafted out into the hallway. The smell was so strong that George was sure the inn was on fire. He escorted Linda to the bottom floor where they located the innkeeper. Upon telling her of their experience, the innkeeper relayed the sad story of Sarah's fate.

The John Rutledge House Inn, circa 1763.

CHARLESTON PLACE HOTEL

This hotel is not an historic building. It first opened September 2, 1986 as the Omni Hotel amid controversy. Eighteenth century homes once stood where the hotel now thrives, but by the 1970s the land had given way to empty storefronts and dilapidated buildings. In 1996, the hotel bought the long boarded up historic Riviera Theatre, which it now uses for special events. For more information, please visit their website at www. charlestonplace.com.

Mischievous Fun

A tired housekeeper, Annie, was walking with a friend down the hall after clocking out at the end of her shift. Annie's friend, Tina was tired from a long day and, as the pair walked and talked, they heard what they thought was a third staff member walking behind them. Because Jim was on the same shift and generally walked with the girls, they thought that it was him who had joined them in the long corridor. Jim was a young man who had told the ladies that there was a ghost that resided in the hallway that he had seen numerous times. The ladies decided to try to scare Jim and quickly ducked into an alcove and waited. As the footsteps drew near, they jumped out to scare their unsuspecting coworker...but no one was there. Frightened, the women hastily left the hotel.

Frightened Apparition

On a stormy night several years ago, Ron was walking down a hall that is not meant for public access. He had worked at the hotel for fifteen years and heard stories and legends that surrounded the building. Although Ron had never experienced anything paranormal himself, he was always cautiously aware of his surroundings. On this particular night, he was walking down an L-shaped hall when he saw a man walking toward him. The man did not look like anyone he knew and in fact appeared to be lost. As Ron greeted him, the man promptly turned and ran down the hall and around the corner. He chased the figure, but when Ron turned the corner the man was gone. Ron immediately reported a suspicious person to the security office, but when an officer reviewed the security tape, Ron was clearly seen running in the hallway...yet no other figure could be found.

Knock, Knock

Ghostly mischief also reigns on the fourth floor of the hotel. Amy was in town for a convention. She normally didn't travel alone, but her husband was in Florida visiting with his father who had just had surgery and work had demanded that she attend the convention. Alone, she turned on the TV and settled in. It wasn't long before she was sleeping. At 2:30 a.m., she woke with a start as someone was knocking on the door. Thinking the TV was keeping her neighbors awake, she turned it off and went to the door prepared to apologize. However, when she opened it, no one was there. Thinking she must have been dreaming, she closed the door. Before her hand moved from the handle, the knocking began again. Startled, she opened the door to an empty hallway. Eventually, she settled back into bed, closing her eyes. Moments later she heard footsteps and a child's laughter. When she opened her eyes, a little boy stood by the edge of her bed. In the shadowy half-light, he looked to be about six years old. She jumped up and turned on the light only to find the room completely empty. Amy immediately packed her things and checked out of the Charleston Place Hotel. It was 4 a.m.

According to the front desk staff, there have been several encounters resulting in guests inexplicably checking out at odd hours. The hotel manager has heard the stories of ghostly encounters from guests and staff alike.

Chapter Six:
CHARLESTON THEATRE GHOSTS

THE RIVIERA THEATRE

The Riviera Theatre opened its doors to an excited audience in 1939. At the time, the theatre was huge and seated 1,193. Its fifty-foot screen delighted moviegoers until 1977. It was leased to a church until the 1980s and then threatened with demolition before being sold to the Charleston Place Hotel. Since then it has been restored and reopened as a conference center and ballroom. But like the hotel, the Riviera was no stranger to ghostly visitors.

A workman spent several days there during renovations. As is the norm, he brought his own tools to the workplace. On this particular day, he spent several hours renovating a room by installing new drywall and woodwork. As he installed a new baseboard, he put his hammer on a worktable directly behind him. When he reached for it again only seconds later, it was gone. Puzzled and frustrated by the end of the day, the worker packed his tools into his truck and left.

When he returned the following morning, the room that he had spent hours working on only the day before was somehow undone. Fresh wood planks were stacked waiting to be cut. Sheets of drywall also lay magically uncut and uninstalled. And there, lying on the worktable was his hammer exactly in the spot where he had placed it the day before.

The Riviera Theatre was built in 1939. Workmen reported paranormal activity during renovations here.

"Spirited" Cleaning

A young bride, along with the typical female members of her wedding party, recently decided to visit the Charleston Place Hotel and was subsequently given a tour of the Riviera Theatre and Conference Center. As she excused herself for a moment to find the ladies' room, she found herself standing in the hallway at the auditorium entrance.

She wasn't sure what caused her to stop. A chill ran up her spine and the little hairs on the back of her neck stood on end. Goose bumps covered her arms. Thinking she was alone, she stood quietly trying to put her finger on the reason for the strange sensations until she heard a scratching sound coming from the auditorium. Sheer curiosity led her to investigate.

As she walked through the door, the sound grew louder. The seats came into view as she rounded a corner and there on the second step between the seats was something she had never witnessed before. The spectral figure of a cleaning woman was busy furiously scrubbing the carpet. The young bride stopped in her tracks when she realized

The small auditorium of the Riviera Theatre... The apparition of a cleaning woman has been seen here.

that the cleaning woman was completely transparent. The scratching sound wafted through the air as the ghostly figure continued with her task...turning a cloth over and over as she scrubbed a stain that couldn't be seen.

DOCK STREET THEATRE

In 1736, America's first theatre was built on Dock Street. Approximately a year later the King was married and Dock Street's name was changed to Queen Street. The theatre thrived until 1809 when it was renovated and became the Planter's Hotel. When Planter's Hotel closed, the building was abandoned until the 1920s when it was renovated again into what was once again known as Dock Street Theatre. The theatre reopened to the public in February 1930 with "The Recruiting Officer," an inspirational comedy.

Christopher Parham, the theatre's manager, doesn't go looking for ghosts. Nonetheless, things have happened at Dock Street Theatre that he hasn't been able to explain. "I have never seen anything," he said. "I have had things move...like change locations and the lights turn off and on without explanation." But Mr. Parham is not convinced that the activity is paranormal.

The theatre has recently undergone a complete renovation. For more information, visit the website www.charlestonstage.com.

Junius Booth

Melissa visited the theatre several years ago to take some photographs for a local newspaper story. She was in the stage area when she heard a noise and turned around to greet who she thought was a theatre employee. When no one was there, she turned back to her task. Again, she heard a noise and turned. Out of the corner of her eye, she noticed a man standing in the balcony. He seemed to be wearing an overcoat, and a top hat. She was going to shout out to greet him, but he evaporated before her eyes.

Many visitors and staff claim to have seen the same man in the balcony. Most believe the apparition to be that of Junius Booth, the father of John Wilkes Booth who assassinated President Lincoln in Washington on April 14, 1865. Junius reputedly was a difficult man. One newspaper article in the Charleston Register depicted the account of Junius beating his manager with an iron rod up and down the hotel halls. He did not kill the man, but came very close.

Nettie and the Unknown Child

A local legend persists concerning a certain young lady named Nettie Dickerson. Nettie worked at the hotel, although her "work" was considered in poor taste. She was a lady of ill-repute during the time that the theatre was a hotel. Legend states that Nettie was on the balcony during a rainstorm when lightning struck, electrocuting her. Her woeful spirit has been seen numerous times over the years all throughout the theatre.

A lesser-known ghost roams the theatre as well. Once, many years ago, Margo was visiting the theatre on a trip with her parents. She was twelve at the time and expressed that she instantly fell in love with Charleston. She was washing her hands in the ladies lounge when she saw the figure of a little girl standing behind her. When she turned around, the child was gone.

THE GARDEN THEATRE

There are several stories repeated in Charleston about the ghostly apparition of young ushers at the local historic theatres. It seems that at a time in the "Old South," when segregation was at its peak, several young African American men met their fate while working as ushers.

A Message from Beyond?

On a hot day in August almost five decades ago, a young man walked down King Street. He whistled as he walked, smiling, and tipping his hat to all he met on the sidewalk. His friendliness was met with glaring hatred. Some even crossed the street to avoid him. He turned left down an alley behind the theatre and entered through a back entrance. There was nothing terribly unusual about him on this particular morning. He was always in a good mood. The

The building that now houses Urban Outfitters was once home to the Garden Theatre.

only difference between him and most of those he met on the street was his skin color. He was a young black man, working as an usher at the Garden Theatre during a time when skin color mattered in the Old South.

The legend of the circumstances that led to his death on that day in the theatre varies. However, one thing is certain. The young man was beaten so severely that he died in seat 108. This is also a mystery as seat 108 was in the section for "whites only" within the theatre. Before the theatre closed in 2002, staff members had reported seeing the apparition of a young black man making his way down the aisles.

On a cool night in 2007, William and his girlfriend were walking along King Street. As they passed by several retail shops, they paused at Urban Outfitters®, which was once the Garden Theatre. They saw a young black man just inside the large storefront window. He stood, mouthing words that the couple, who were just inches from the glass, could not hear. The couple turned to each other to see if one another could make out what the young man was saying, but when they turned back, "…he was fading. He became transparent and then just disappeared, still trying to tell us something."

Could the spirit of a young black man still be haunting the building that was once known as the Garden Theatre? There are some who don't think so. They believe his spirit traveled a little over a mile south, with the seat he reportedly died in, to a small pizza place located within the old Rainbow Market.

Pizzeria Di Giovanni's

On one of our visits to Charleston, my husband and I decided to eat at Pizzeria Di Giovanni's in the Rainbow Market. We had just finished a ghost tour and to our surprise the restaurant is open until 4 a.m. on the weekends. It had been a long day of research and interviews. Pizza sounded good.

Theatre seats from the Garden Theatre... Local legend states that an usher died in one of these seats.

We placed our order and took a seat at a table by the wall. As we talked about the day and the various ghost stories and historical facts that are in abundance in Charleston, I couldn't shake the feeling of being watched. At the time the restaurant was not very crowded. As we talked, a man at the table next to us overheard our conversation and began to tell us that he and his wife also had some strange sensations from the moment they entered the restaurant.

As things happen, we ended up sitting at a table with our newfound friends. We were discussing all things haunted when the server brought our pizza. Overhearing us, he politely asked if we would speak with the owner. My curiosity was peaked and I couldn't wait to hear what the owner had to say. Encouraged by his staff, the reluctant owner came over to the table. After brief introductions, he began to tell me of some of the things happening at the restaurant.

He said that during renovations, everything seemed fine. He knew the history of the building and had joked with some of the locals about Charleston ghosts. He wasn't sure what was happening, but admitted to some bizarre events that began only a few days before our visit that night.

One morning, as he was tidying up after a long night's work, he heard the sound of someone talking in the back room. He was startled and annoyed because he knew no one else should have been in the restaurant, as he had sent everyone home. When he went to investigate the source of the voices, the restaurant was empty.

On another occasion, he was working on some of the equipment inside the restaurant. As he worked, he laid his tools out on the counter. One of the soda machines was being particularly stubborn and he ended up needing to squat down to attempt to loosen a bolt. When he reached for the wrench that he knew was on the counter just above his head, he couldn't find it. He stood up and looked for the tool, but it had completely disappeared — twenty minutes later, it reappeared on the counter exactly in the spot where he had left it.

It seems that only days before, the owner had moved several original seats from the Garden Theatre into the restaurant. He purchased them from a local Charlestonian who had acquired the seats after the last renovation. Hoping they would add to the ambience, he placed the seats on a loft within the restaurant. Other staff members have said that they smell popcorn at various times throughout their shift when no popcorn has been made. They attribute the smell to the Garden Theatre seats and greet their new inhabitant with a friendly "hello." Be sure to plan a visit. Giovanni's is located at 40 North Market Street and they can be contacted at 843-727-6767.

Chapter Seven:

RESIDENTIAL GHOSTS

LEGARE STREET GHOSTS

The Chisolm House
23 Legare Street

Once home to writer Herbert Ravenal Sass, this circa 1838 home was built by Dr. Robert Trail Chisolm. At the front of the house is a set of beautiful iron gates so prominent in Charleston. These particular gates are said to date to 1817.

More than a century later a member of the Chisolm family was researching the old house when they asked permission from the owners to tour it. As the young man walked up the staircase, he was greeted by what appeared to be an older gentleman. The man was standing on the landing of the stairs. He looked to be in his early 50's and was wearing what appeared to be a close fitting vest and overcoat. When the young man greeted the spectral figure, he smiled and then disappeared. The ghost seems to only show itself to members of the Chisolm family.

Heyward House
31 Legare Street

On a quiet morning in 1805, Mrs. Heyward was sitting in her library. She looked up from her needlework to see her son, James, standing near the fireplace. He was dressed in his hunting clothes. His face appeared to be very pale and he had a troubled look. Hannah Heyward asked her son what was wrong...he evaporated before her eyes.

Later that day Hannah received the news that James was on a hunting expedition when he accidentally fired his rifle, shooting himself in the neck. The bullet struck his jugular and he died almost instantly. The time of his death was the exact moment that he appeared in front of his mother in the library.

The ghost has been seen numerous times over the years. He is always in the library sometimes standing near the window, but most often he appears to be reading a book.

Mrs. Heyward's daughter allowed the house to be used as a private school for ladies from 1830 to 1837. Augustine Smythe bought the property in 1870 and the house remains in his family to this day.

The Ghost of Madame Tavande
39 Legare Street

On a cool day in 1996, Samantha was walking with her sister down Legare Street. As they walked, they admired the beautiful seventeenth century homes. As they approached the house at 39 Legare Street, the women heard the sound of approaching hooves. Thinking a carriage was coming up behind them, they turned to watch. Only modern vehicles graced the street. The sisters stood in awe and then turned their attention back to the house. They noticed a woman peering down at them from an upstairs window.

Ann Marson Talvande's family were refugees during the Haitian revolution. In typical French fashion, after her arrival in Charleston, Madame Talvande took note of her abilities and promptly opened a girl's school at 32 Legare Street in 1810. She was a woman of small stature, caring for her students but also reigning with a strict hand and a quick temper.

Colonel Joseph Whaley had a problem — his beautiful fourteen-year-old daughter, Maria. More specifically, the problem was the man whose romantic intentions were directed at Maria. Like most fathers, Colonel Whaley was very protective of his daughter. When he asked George Norris to take his attentions elsewhere, the young man responded by pitching a tent next to Colonel Whaley's Pine Barren Plantation on Edisto Island.

The Sword Gates are located on Legare Street.

Maria's mother had passed away when she was only eight. Although Colonel Whaley had remarried, he felt that Maria would benefit from a strict hand and a proper education and, in 1828, thought he had a solution when he enrolled Maria in Madame Talvande's School for Girls. The school was in Charleston, away from the island. There, he thought that Maria could focus on her studies and the attentions of the young man would soon fade away. Poor Colonel Whaley was wrong.

On a rainy night in March 1828, George Norris paced back and forth at St. Michael's Church. He anxiously awaited the arrival of his bride-to-be. Soon, he heard the sound of an approaching carriage. A brief but romantic ceremony bonded Maria and her beloved. The married couple rode in a coach back to the school where they exchanged a kiss before saying goodnight.

The following morning, the dashing young man came to the school to collect his bride. Madame Talvande, embarrassed by the situation, soon erected a brick wall and an iron gate to deter suitors from eloping with her students. Colonel Whaley, resigned to the fact that his daughter was happily married, soon forgave Maria and her new husband.

Several visitors to Charleston have spotted the faint apparition of a woman roaming the upstairs rooms at 39 Legare Street. Some have speculated that it could be Madame Talvande searching the halls, forever checking on her students. Although the school closed in 1848, a new brick wing and subsequent gate were added on the premises in 1849. The new gate has come to be known as the Sword Gate. The intricate iron gate was made in 1838 by Christopher Werner and he is said to still haunt his gate, not wanting to allow anyone in — or out.

THE GHOST ON TRADD STREET

Becky, Todd, Wendy, and Brad arrived in Charleston on a Thursday afternoon. Becky's aunt was the owner of a beautiful home on Tradd Street and Becky and her husband, along with their best friends, were house-sitting while her aunt vacationed in Europe. After enjoying a wonderful dinner on the town, the four sat around an antique table in the formal dining room playing cards. As the night wore on, the conversation turned to the many ghost tours in Charleston and the possibility that the old house might be haunted. Before long, Brad suggested a séance.

Soon, candlelight was casting a warm yellow-orange glow all around them. Todd instructed the friends to join hands and close their eyes. As he spoke, the four seemed to relax. After a short prayer for protection, Todd continued, "We ask that you communicate with us." Silence. "We ask that you rap on the table, or touch one of us." Nothing. After an hour, they gave up and retired to bed.

Becky curled up with her husband. They were "spooning" as she drifted off to sleep. The buzzing whir of the air conditioner crept into her dream. It was getting louder and louder. They were all back at the table again. This time, though, there was something else there...something unseen.

In her dream, Becky was watching herself from afar. As Todd attempted in vain to communicate, a gray shape took form in the corner. It was just a shadow at first, flickering in the candlelight, but soon, it began to grow larger. Moments later, it was the distinct shape of a man and it moved between the table where Becky was sitting and the window. When it reached her aunt's antique hutch, it stopped. The form seemed to pulse and glow as a shadowy arm reached for a shining silver cake knife and threw it. The knife was sailing through the air. In her dream, Becky's view suddenly changed and she noticed the knife when it was about a foot from her face. When she opened her mouth to scream, it landed gently in her mouth. At first she was afraid to move. She could taste the metal, but then she gently pulled the knife from her lips, amazed that she wasn't even nicked.

The sound of the fan was growing loud. The whirring buzz vibrated Becky's head as she slowly came out of her deep slumber. Once she realized that she had been dreaming, the full extent of her fear overwhelmed her and tears welled up in her eyes. She gently stroked her husband's arm, failing to arouse him from his own apparent nightmare.

Knowing sleep would not return quickly, she quietly got out of bed and put on her robe. She cringed every time the boards creaked as she walked down the old stairs. When she finally reached the bottom, she sighed in relief. On her way to the parlor, she passed by the dining room, where her relief turned to terror — the knife from her dream was now resting on the table where she had been seated earlier in the evening!

MEETING STREET APPARITIONS

On a quiet fall morning in 1858, sixteen-year-old John Blake was supposed to go hunting. Instead, he lay in his bed with a fever and a massive headache. His worried father left to retrieve the doctor, and the two were hurriedly making their way back to the Meeting Street residence. John had never felt this sick before. His mother was wiping the boy with cool wet cloth strips to help calm his raging fever. Unfortunately, John Blake lost his life on October 14, 1858 to Yellow Fever. By now, the epidemic had swarmed Charleston and more than 2,000 residents had succumbed to the illness.

Panic was widespread. As city officials tried to find a cause, one of the cited reasoning for the outbreak was the burial ground beneath the city. Other reasons included poor ventilation, drains, and sewers. Nearly a hundred years later scientific research would determine that Yellow Fever was actually viral and spread by mosquitoes. The disease got its name due to the yellowing of the eyes and skin of those afflicted.

On the cool fall morning of October 14, 2000, Gregg finished his shower and walked into the second floor bedroom at his Meeting Street home wearing only a towel. He stopped when he noticed a strange reflection in the mirror. There appeared to be a teenaged boy lying in his bed. In the reflection he could clearly see a woman wringing out a cloth and placing it on the boy's head. Gregg turned his eyes to the bed, where he saw nothing, and then back to the reflection in the mirror. The woman looked up from her patient and seemed to see Gregg, who was suddenly embarrassed. He took a step backward as the ghostly scene faded. His reflection was all that remained. He nervously dressed and left the house.

Since this interview took place a few years after the incident, I asked Gregg how he could be certain of the date and he stated that he had been getting ready that morning to pick up his girlfriend for a trip to her parents' home on St. John's Island to celebrate her birthday.

FIRE STATION AND POLICE PHANTOMS

Most of us go about our daily lives knowing that in the case of a real emergency, help is only a phone call away. The men and women who respond to our cries for help are everyday heroes. My research in Charleston led me to interview several off-duty firefighters, police officers, and associates. This particular group of people was reluctant to share, but were profoundly affected by their experiences and desperately searching for answers. While their stories are relayed in

One of the historic fire stations in Charleston.

this book as they were told to me, the names have been changed to protect the people's identities and specific location information is vague. Please do not approach Police and Fire personnel while they are on duty to inquire about paranormal activity. Answering your questions concerning ghosts and hauntings could distract them from saving someone's life.

Mischief

Bill had been assigned to a fire station in Charleston that is notorious for the paranormal activity. He had heard stories from his comrades about the phantom that plays tricks on the firefighters, but Bill didn't believe in ghosts. Then he arrived for his first 24-hour shift at the fire station... Let's just say, he believes in them now.

After an uneventful day, the firefighters retired to their sleeping quarters. As the hours wore on, the station became eerily quiet. Bill was trying to sleep, but couldn't. After a failed attempt to lull himself into a slumber by reading, he gave up and went downstairs to watch TV. Not wanting to disturb his comrades, he didn't turn on the lights inside the station and kept the TV volume low.

Outside the streetlights cast a glow into the room. Bill had gotten himself a snack and settled back in to watch some late night show. A few minutes later, he had the unmistakable feeling of being watched. When the feeling didn't subside, he turned to focus on the stairs behind him. There, at the top of the stairs was a black mass. As it moved down the staircase, Bill realized that the mass was not transparent. It was solid and shapeless. It took no defining form as it moved.

Bill blinked and looked away. When he looked back, the black mass was gone. Convinced that his comrades had played some kind of strange trick on him, Bill ran up the stairs to catch them in the act. When he reached the top, there was no one or nothing there — no black mass and no giggling firefighters. As he checked each room, he found that all of his comrades were sound asleep.

The "insomniac event" was not the only strange occurrence to happen to Bill at the fire station. After returning from a call, Bill went to take a shower. At this particular fire station there is only one entrance into the showers. The entrance is off the exercise room and through two sets of doors. Bill locked the first door and then the second so that no one would inadvertently walk in on him as he was showering.

As hot water cascaded down his back, Bill thought he heard something and peered through the glass toward the door. He saw a fleeting form and said out loud, "I'll be done in a few minutes." When he was dressed, he went to leave the shower area and just as he suspected the first door was unlocked. However, he was stunned to discover that the second door — the one that led to the exercise room — remained locked. No one had entered the shower area.

Other paranormal events that take place at the fire station include flickering lights and objects that disappear and reappear in the most interesting places — like lost keys showing up in the refrigerator. There is a rumor that persists concerning this particular fire station. Years ago a fire chief reportedly was dabbling in Satanism. The chief habitually performed satanic rituals on the grounds of the fire station and at times, even in his own sleeping quarters. The story most often reported is that the chief was performing rituals in his room when he ran into the hallway screaming, "Don't let them get me!" The chief reportedly retired shortly after that event so many years ago.

It is hard for me to imagine a satanic fire chief. I have to admit I don't know much about this particular religion. However, it's hard for me to reconcile a desire to help save lives with worshipping such a dark and evil entity.

RIP

Another fire station located in the historic district offers some interesting phenomenon as well. A fire fighter we'll call "Tom" shared the following story:

At first, the fire was manageable. The fire was stubborn, though. It took several hours to tame the blazes before finally putting the fire completely out. As the firefighters returned to the station, they were exhausted…and hungry. After washing up, they gathered in the station's kitchen where a meal was being prepared. A lull in the conversation produced an unnatural quiet. That's when they heard her. She was singing a lullaby.

The sound of her lovely voice was coming from the second floor just above the kitchen. After calling out and hearing no response — other than the dreamlike singing — the firefighters decided to go upstairs and confront the soulful intruder. At the top of the stairs, the air began to cool. A flickering glow was oozing into the hallway from one of the rooms above the kitchen. "Hello." No response. The first firefighter to reach the room placed his hand on the door to push it open and abruptly stopped. He described the room as changed somehow. He said it was transformed. A fireplace was the source of the glow and a woman stood in the corner holding a toddler who appeared to be sleeping. He could see the child's tiny feet as she swayed, her long dark hair spilling over the woman's arm. The woman holding her continued to sing as she rocked the child back and forth, a small smile of contentment spread over her lips. She took a step forward as her gaze rose from the child to the door. She suddenly stopped singing and stared at the firefighters now standing in the room… and disappeared.

The room was suddenly empty. No fireplace and no warm glow spilling into the hallway. The singing had stopped and the woman, along with the toddler and the furnishings, was also gone. The firefighters were alarmed when they realized that all three of them had seen the same vision of the woman and the toddler. Over the next few days the firefighters were diligent in their search for an answer. Historical records indicated that the station was, indeed, once a private residence.

Did the firefighters witness a ghost? Or did they somehow open a window to the past and cross the time barrier to reach out to a mysterious woman and a sleeping toddler?

Answering the Call

I wondered how long Charleston's police and firefighters had been witnessing strange apparitions and paranormal phenomena in one of our nation's oldest cities. By chance, I had the privilege of meeting and subsequently interviewing a retired associate who worked with the police department. I began by asking him how many times he had heard stories involving ghosts or hauntings from his associates while at work. The answer was surprising: "At least once a month." As we continued the conversation, he relayed the following extraordinary stories.

A Ghostly Intruder

The year was 1971. On a relatively quiet night, Officers Ron and Dave had just finished a quick bite to eat. As Officer Ron sipped his root beer, the call came from dispatch to respond to a 10-15 (disturbance) at a private residence in the historic district.

When the officers arrived, the house was dark. A middle-aged woman answered the door and immediately pushed her finger to her lips signaling the officers to remain quiet. Her hair was long and gray, pulled back into a loose ponytail. She was small, only about five feet tall. Her shiny blue eyes were wide with fear. Just as Officer Ron was about to speak, she pointed to the upstairs and motioned the men inside. As they entered the residence they realized that someone was running back and forth above them in the upstairs hallway. The footsteps were heavy and seemed to pause briefly here and there with no rhyme or reason. The middle-aged woman introduced herself as "Kathy." She motioned toward a room near the foyer where an elderly woman was laying on a hospital bed. "This is my Mother," she whispered. Suddenly footfalls thundered above them. Kathy explained that she and her Mother had been watching TV when suddenly there was a noise upstairs — like something heavy falling on the floor. Footsteps immediately followed and grew increasingly louder. Frightened, Kathy called the police. "Officer," she whispered. "This is not a break-in. There is no outside entrance to the upstairs rooms. There's not even a fire escape. Whoever is up there had to be hiding since Sunday. I haven't left the house since then."

Officer Ron stood at the base of the stairs. He hoped to be able to see the intruder from his position. As the footsteps rang out across the upstairs hallway, the stairs vibrated. Yet he didn't see anything. Officer Dave joined him near the bottom of the stairs. The officers paused and listened. A few minutes later, they decided that it sounded as if there was only one intruder. No voices were heard. Only one pair of feet could be heard screaming across the upstairs floor. Officer Ron began to ascend the trembling staircase.

As he made his way to the top of the stairs, he called out. The thundering footsteps immediately stopped. The Officer was sure that whoever had been running across the hallway floor had suddenly decided it was best to hide. Officer Dave guarded the stairs so that the perpetrator would have no escape. As Officer Ron checked each of the upstairs rooms, he realized with growing panic that no one was there. The drawers and furnishings were intact. Nothing had been disturbed. It appeared that whoever it was wasn't searching for anything of value to steal. The house was empty except for Kathy and her mother.

Officer Ron spent several hours at the house that day. He and Officer Dave had scoured the home and surrounding grounds. Kathy had been right. There was no way for someone to reach the upper floor without entering the home from the first level. The windows also remained locked from the inside. Even if someone had found a way to exit from one of the top floor windows (managing to close and re-lock it afterward) and jump to the ground, the fall would most certainly have caused an injury.

Strange goings-on continued at the house for several weeks until Kathy turned to her church for help. A local priest blessed the home, but the activity never stopped completely until a few months later. On Christmas Eve, Kathy's mother turned to her and whispered, "Aunt Rosa is here," before quietly passing away. "Rosa had been dead for seventeen years," he said, his face turning white even now as he relayed the story. Whatever resided at the residence never returned after that day.

First Response

Officer Jeff was patrolling his route along the waterfront on the northeast side of Charleston — the same route he had been patrolling for the last seven years. The fall air was cold especially along the waterfront. As the night wore on, Jeff drummed his fingers on the steering wheel and hummed a favorite tune. As he passed by a streetlight, he noticed a woman pushing a baby in an antique stroller on the sidewalk overlooking the river. There are many wealthy antique collectors in Charleston. It was a perfectly normal thing to see...had it not been 2 a.m. His first instinct was to stop the woman and make sure that everything was okay, but then he remembered how his own son had kept him and his wife awake during those first few months. Many nights his wife would leave with the baby safely secured in the car seat. The car ride would inevitably lull the infant to sleep. Jeff decided to wave to the woman as he passed by. She waved back and continued pushing the stroller down the sidewalk.

Satisfied that all was well, Jeff continued on his route. An hour later he was surprised when he passed by the same spot and the woman was still strolling with the baby. Now concerned that something must be wrong as he couldn't imagine keeping a baby out in the cold night air, he decided to stop and check on them. As he approached, he noticed that the woman was now standing gazing into the murky water with the infant in her arms. Jeff was alarmed. He watched in horror as she stepped onto the sea wall and prepared to jump. She stopped, clutching the tiny infant in her arms. As Jeff began to approach her, he noticed that she was wearing a 1920s beaded dress and a fur lined wrap-around coat. She turned toward him, tears streaming down her face, and disappeared. She didn't jump — she simply faded away. The antique stroller that had been on the sidewalk only a few feet from where the officer now stood was also gone.

~~~~~

Author's Note: I could find nothing in the historic records in Charleston that suggested a woman was saved from suicide along the waterfront, but perhaps decades ago, on a cold fall night, someone came across a despondent woman and her baby and saved them.

Chapter Eight:

ISLAND GHOSTS

KIAWAH ISLAND GHOSTS

Kiawah Island lies approximately twenty-six miles southeast from Charleston. Like all of the local islands, Kiawah has born witness to the Revolutionary and Civil wars. Soldiers from every side have marched across its shores. In 1775, Arnoldus Vanderhorst built a cotton and indigo plantation on Kiawah Island. The British burned the plantation to the ground in 1780. By 1802, the plantation was rebuilt. During the Civil War, the home was all but demolished by Union troops. Arnoldus Vanderhorst IV rebuilt the plantation and began growing cotton. In 1880, Arnoldus Vanderhorst IV was accidentally killed when he fell into a ditch discharging his gun. In 1994, a private investor bought the property and began restoration of the former plantation house. Resilience is a word that comes to mind when I think about this plantation home…and its occupants.

Spring is especially a beautiful time on the islands. A visitor to the island was riding a bike. Enroute he encountered a strangely dressed man who was walking along the road. As he approached, the man slowed down his stride and turned toward the biker, who stopped when he realized the man was carrying an antique gun. The man spoke with a low tone asking for help in figuring out his whereabouts. The confused biker informed the man that he was on Kiawah Island at which point the strange man rolled his eyes and said, "Sir, I am aware of which island I stand on. I have simply misplaced my hunting party. Good day." With that, the man disappeared. The perplexed biker never made it to the beach that day. Instead he returned to his hotel, packed his things, and left the island.

Another visitor to the island was actually staying at the Vanderhorst Mansion several years ago when he encountered what he believed to

The Vanderhorst Mausoleum is located at Magnolia Cemetery in Charleston.

be the ghost of a cat. "I reached down to pet it and it backed away from me and hissed before disappearing into a wall." Several other Vanderhorst Mansion visitors have experienced not only the ghostly cat, but also the spirit of a little boy. The child supposedly died while searching for his missing cat.

EDISTO ISLAND

Ghostly legends are persistent throughout Charleston. Like all legends, these ghostly tales are based in fact. The following legends have been told often. Margaret Rhett Martin first wrote the legend of Brick House in 1963 in her book Charleston Ghosts. Although we may never know the true identity of Amelia or the manner in which she died, there are some interesting facts that remain.

Amelia's Story

The following is from Margaret Martin's book:

Amelia came to live at Brick House Plantation with the Jenkins family. The reasons are unclear, but it seems her parents hoped for the upbringing that they knew her extended family could provide. Amelia, like most children, was quick to make friends. She spent her days wandering the island, playing games, fishing, and climbing trees. One of her closest friends was a Native American boy named Concha. Through the years, Amelia and Concha became inseparable. When Concha stopped by to play, he would call for Amelia from the woods with a birdcall. As time went by, Amelia grew into a beautiful young lady. Her reputation in the community was that she was very sweet and smart. Concha had grown too — and he realized that he loved Amelia more than anyone he had ever met.

As was the custom of the day, on Amelia's eighteenth birthday, a grand party was planned. She wore a beautiful dress and long white gloves. As Amelia readied for the party, she heard the familiar call from the woods and hurried down the stairs to greet her friend. Concha took Amelia by the hand and proclaimed his love for her. Then on bended knee, he asked Amelia to be his wife.

Amelia was heartbroken. She loved Concha, but as a friend. She knew that her family would never accept Concha as her husband. She told Concha that she did not love him in that way and turned to finish preparing for her party. Concha called out to her and proclaimed that he would never allow her to marry a white man. Amelia watched in disbelief as Concha, riddled with rage, fled into the woods. Amelia returned to her bedroom where she mourned the loss of her best friend. When she heard guests arriving for her party, she wiped her tears away and straightened her beautiful gown. She joined her guests and it wasn't long before she forgot all about Concha.

One of the guests at the party was a striking young man named Paul Grimball. Amelia noticed him almost immediately. His family had a plantation nearby and he was considered one of the most respectable bachelors on the island. When Paul saw Amelia, he knew his heart was lost forever. The two danced all night. Before long, they were spending long days together on the island. Soon, they announced their engagement.

On the day of her wedding, Amelia was getting ready in her upstairs bedroom. She was beautiful in a flowing gown and had her veil pinned back covering her beautiful long locks. As she was primping, she heard a familiar birdcall from outside. She went to the window and saw Concha standing in the yard. She turned, not wanting to speak to him on her wedding day, and heard the whoosh of an arrow. She screamed as it struck her chest. She began to walk down the stairs as her beloved Paul rushed up to meet her. He carried her to the thirteenth step and stumbled, holding Amelia in his arms. There her blood drained from her body as she died in the arms of her true love.

Amelia's Story, Part II

Another legend of how Amelia may have met her fate was written by Geordie Buxton in his book Haunted Plantations (Buxton, 2007) and goes something like this:

Amelia was betrothed to a man from a wealthy family in Charleston. The man gave her a beautiful ring. The ring was extravagant even for the elite Charlestonians of the day. Amelia would flaunt the ring whenever she was given a chance. As time went by, Amelia met another man at a dinner party near Edisto Island, where she lived. The man commented on how her ring reminded him of one his grandmother wore and the pair instantly fell in love. She wrote to her betrothed in Charleston explaining to him that she was not in love with him and requested that their engagement be dissolved.

Not wanting to lose Amelia, her betrothed rode out to her home on Edisto Island and demanded an explanation. He begged and pleaded with Amelia, but her mind — and her heart — was made up and she sent the young man away. Before he left, he swore to her that she would never marry another man. A few years later, on her wedding night, Amelia was in her upstairs bedroom preparing for the ceremony. As guests began to arrive, Amelia heard the sound of a familiar voice calling her from downstairs. She opened the window and saw her former fiancé standing in the yard with a pistol aimed at her. She screamed too late as a single shot rang out. Amelia's beloved rushed up the stairs to find her already dead in a puddle of blood.

Maybe Not A Legend Afterall

Brick House burned down in 1929. All that stands today are the brick walls, but it is said that on clear nights Amelia's ghost can be seen in the upstairs window. A strange birdcall from the woods and a shrill scream pierce the night air. There is then the sound of heavy footsteps on the long-gone stairs.

Brick House was built in 1725 by Paul Hamilton. After changing hands several times, by 1798 the Jenkins family bought the plantation and it remains in the family today. The site is a registered historical landmark and a fine architectural example of the "double house" that was popular in Charleston in the 1750s and 1760s. Permission to visit Brick House should be requested through the Edisto Island Historic Preservation Society.

It is interesting to note that I was able to find one Paul Chaplin Grimball in the historic archives of Charleston County on Edisto Island. He was born in 1788 and married a widow, Elizabeth Jenkins, in 1814. He was twenty-six at the time. Elizabeth was born in 1763. It is not a hard stretch to imagine that he would have become close with the Jenkins family and ended up courting and marrying a Jenkins girl after the death of his beloved Amelia.

JOHN'S ISLAND

Not too far from Angel Oak on John's Island is an area known as Bloody Dick Swamp. The area is a marshland surrounded by woods and therefore a nature lover's paradise. Kevin and his girlfriend were driving along the old road when something happened that would change them forever. Kevin carried a secret tucked away in his shirt pocket. As he parked the car and turned toward his girlfriend, Carrie, he nervously took her hand in his and began to speak. "You know I love you. I can't imagine my life without you."

Carrie screamed. She was looking beyond Kevin out the driver's side window. Kevin turned to look in the same direction when he saw a man standing by the car. The man was dressed in a Confederate uniform and was covered in blood. He had a stern look on his face and stared at the frightened couple.

Carrie begged Kevin to leave, but when he turned the key in the ignition, the car wouldn't start. A strange charge was in the air as the soldier walked slowly from the driver side to the passenger side. The hair on the back of Kevin's neck stood on end. Carrie screamed again. As Kevin tried furiously to start the car, the soldier reached a bloody hand toward Carrie and disappeared. Kevin put the car in reverse, turned around, and sped toward the main road.

A while later, the weary couple arrived at a nearby restaurant. After nervously laughing off the sighting of the apparition, Kevin pulled a diamond ring from his pocket and proposed to Carrie. The two were married less than a year later. The bloody Confederate soldier apparition has been spotted along the swamp numerous times. Some accounts say that the soldier creeps or crawls from the water. One common fact is that the soldier seems to be angry and elicits a sense of foreboding to all who see him.

SULLIVAN'S ISLAND

The Ghost of Edgar Allan Poe

As 26-year-old Carly Jones walked along the beach on Sullivan's Island on a beautiful summer morning in 2005, among carefree families playing in the sand and surf, she was looking for shells. Seeing a pink glimmer jutting out of the sand, she reached down and picked up an unusual specimen. She had visited the island many times before, but had never seen a shell like this. It was pink and rough on the outside with a smooth dark burgundy color on the inside. She slid the shell in her pocket and continued her morning walk. A little further down the beach she noticed another pink shell and leaned over to pick it up. She took the other shell from her pocket and stood transfixed, turning them in the bright sunshine and comparing their size and color when a young man approached her. He had long dark hair and dark eyes. At first, he seemed troubled, but then when he began to speak there was a certain calm and friendly demeanor about him that put Carly at ease. He told Carly about the shells and how many different species could be found on the island. He explained where the pink hue came from and how rare it is to find such a specimen. He spoke with enthusiasm and was very polite. Carly was still looking at the shells as the young man walked away. Realizing she had forgotten to thank him, she looked up only to see that he had disappeared.

Later that night, Carly was enjoying dinner at a local restaurant with her boyfriend. As she looked around, she noticed a picture on the wall of the young man who had joined her on the beach. Inquiring about his identity, she was informed that the young man in the picture was Edgar Allan Poe.

History of a Great American Writer

Elizabeth Poe arrived in Charleston in January 1811. She performed at a local theatre with three small children in tow: William Henry, Edgar Allan, and Rosalie. David Poe had abandoned his family in late 1809. By autumn of 1811, Elizabeth's health was failing. She died December 8. William returned to his grandfather's home in Baltimore, but the youngest orphans (Rosalie and Edgar) were placed in foster care. Edgar ended up in the home of John and Frances Valentine Allan. Although he lived with the couple for many years, they never formally adopted him. He was given the name Edgar "Allan" Poe through his baptism in 1812 at the Episcopal Church in Richmond.

Edgar attended various schools in Richmond and eventually studied at various boarding schools in his foster father's hometown in Scotland. Later, he enrolled in the University of Virginia. It was there that Poe incurred a large amount of gambling debts and eventually withdrew. Edgar's withdrawal led to a bitter argument between himself and John Allan, his foster father. Finding himself without means of support, Edgar enrolled in the U.S. Army under the name Edgar A. Perry and found himself on the way to South Carolina's Fort Moultrie in early 1827.

During his station at Fort Moultrie, Poe was well liked and became fast friends with a local conchologist and professor, Dr. Edmund Ravenel. An avid shell collector, Ravenel was known to wander the beaches on Sullivan's Island where he kept a home. While there is no hard proof that Ravenel and Poe searched the beaches for shells together, it would be difficult to imagine that these friends wouldn't share some conversations on the topic as they shared a common interest and lived on the same small island. Alas, Poe's stay at Fort Moultrie would be short-lived. It wasn't long before he realized that military life really didn't agree with him. He wanted to pursue his writing career.

On December 1, 1828, Poe wrote to John Allan. In that correspondence he informed his estranged foster father that he had a deep desire to leave the military and pursue a writing career. He went on to say that he had talked the matter over with his Lieutenant who informed him that he would only give him an honorable discharge if he could reconcile with his foster father. Poe had initially resisted, informing the Lieutenant that his foster father had loved him and would want only the best for him. The Lieutenant obviously had the young Poe's best interest at heart when he insisted that he write his foster father. Poe threatened to take more drastic measures should his foster father be unwilling to help with his plight. After more correspondence between himself and his estranged foster father,

Poe would be transferred to West Point and from there discharged from the U.S. Army. He had been promoted twice during his station on Sullivan's Island, reaching the highest rank of Sergeant Major for an enlisted man.

There's no doubt that Poe would have heard the stories of pirates and ghostly apparitions as well as the rich folklore that had permeated the low country during his stay on Sullivan's Island. Tales of voodoo, misty swamps, and local legends made their way into Poe's writings, including The Gold Bug. Perhaps because his time at Fort Moultrie was one of the most stable times of his life, Poe seemed to carry Sullivan's Island with him. Edgar Allan Poe was found wandering the streets of Baltimore, delirious and in clothes that did not belong to him on October 3, 1849. Never regaining his senses, he died October 7, 1849 in Baltimore, Maryland. Poe is said to have called out the name "Reynolds" repeatedly on the night when he died. The exact cause of his death is unknown. He was forty years old.

Phantom Fish at the Lighthouse

Sullivan's Island Lighthouse isn't what typical tourists expect to see. There's no familiar round shape. There's no romantic story. Instead, the three-sided lighthouse resembles a modern aircraft control tower. The lightkeepers never had to climb a winding staircase, but rather hopped in an elevator and enjoyed a leisurely ride to the top. There, they would finish the ascent with a climb up a steep 25-foot ladder to the lantern room. The summer sun never bothered them much either, as the lighthouse is air-conditioned. The lighthouse began operating in 1962. On the same grounds, a lifesaving station was built in 1898. The buildings and accompanying boathouse remain today and are used as offices for the Coast Guard and National Park Service.

Several years ago Paul, a National Park Service employee, was quietly working at his desk inside the old building when he smelled the unmistakable scent of fish and salt water. Thinking this really wasn't that unusual (after all, he was only steps from the ocean), he simply returned his attention back to work. A few moments later he heard what sounded like a door opening and something being pulled across a wooden floor. The sound was emanating from the front door.

Certain that another employee had come in, he called out, "Do you need some help?" No one answered. He stood from his desk and walked out to the foyer. When he didn't find anyone there, he searched the entire building. Still finding no one and thinking they must have gone back outside, he searched the lighthouse grounds. There was nobody else on the grounds. Puzzled, he returned to the old building and walked through the front door. There, on the floor was a puddle of water and a flapping live fish. He stood in amazement, wondering who would bring a fish into the building and leave it on the floor. As he bent down to pick the flapping fish up, it vanished.

Paul jerked his hand back and stood transfixed staring at the floor. It was dry. The fish was gone. Frightened, he slowly walked back to his desk and phoned his wife to relay the spooky experience. Paul never encountered another phantom fish, but said that other employees had made reports of hearing strange sounds and voices when no one else was in the building.

Chapter Nine:

PIRATES, PATRIOTS, AND THE GULLAHS

WHITE POINT GARDENS

On the waterfront in Charleston is a beautiful park called White Point Gardens. As lovers stroll by holding hands and children play, it's hard to imagine the dark history that occurred there.

Ghostly Pirates

Richard Worley

On a cool night in April, Margaret was walking along the waterfront at White Point Gardens with her husband. The full moon loomed overhead cascading a myriad of reflections on the water. They were enjoying the night air when suddenly Margaret

White Point Gardens... This site is where many executions are said to have taken place.

saw something out of the corner of her eye. She turned and her husband followed suit. There a shadowy figure appeared. The apparition was a hanging man, swaying in the moonlight. The man, dressed in stockings, breeches, white shirt, and vest, was hanging from a rope. Following the rope upward, the couple realized that there were no gallows. The man seemed to be suspended in mid-air.

More than two centuries before on a cold September morning Richard Worley stepped onto a small boat in New York with seven other men. The boat was not seaworthy, so the men headed south and captured a better boat on the Delaware River. This was an act of burglary under maritime law because it didn't occur on the open seas. Their next criminal act was one of piracy as the crew took over a sailing ship and added four more members to the crew, bringing the number to twelve.

As they made their way south, King George I issued a proclamation against pirates who had not accepted the royal pardon from British government. The royal warship Phoenix was sent to capture Worley and his crew, to no avail. Six weeks later, off the coast of the Bahamas, Worley had captured two more vessels and began flying his official flag — the skull and crossbones. Within a few weeks, Worley and his crew, which had grown to a fleet and several men, began to trek north. In North Carolina, Worley's fleet was busy refitting their ships. When the Governor heard about this, he sent two war vessels after them. At the mouth of Jamestown Harbor, Worley and his crew mistook the vessels for two merchant vessels. Maneuvering into the harbor to prevent the vessels from entering, Worley inadvertently trapped his own ship, resulting in its easy capture.

When the authorities attempted to board Worley's vessel, the men fought to the death. Only Worley and one other crewmember survived. They were convicted of piracy and sentenced to death the next day. Other accounts claim that up to twenty-five of Worley's crew was also sentenced to death. In any case, Worley and what was left of his crew were hanged at White Point Gardens on February 17, 1719.

Blackbeard and Stede Bonnet

Stede Bonnet was the son of wealthy plantation owners in Barbados. After possibly serving in the King's army during the war with Spain, he returned to Barbados where he married and inherited his father's plantation in 1694. He was a wealthy landowner who, in the summer of 1717, left a perfectly normal life in Barbados to pursue a life of crime as a pirate.

Some say that marital issues are what drove Bonnet to purchase a sloop, which he named "the Revenge" and outfitted with ten cannons. Then, he proceeded to do something that no other pirate had ever done before. Stede Bonnet hired a crew. The men were paid wages instead of a percentage of their plunder. This was unheard of and earned Bonnet the nickname "the gentleman pirate."

In Nassau, after a raid in which he was injured, Bonnet met the legendary Edward Teach, also known as Blackbeard. There Bonnet surrendered his vessel to Teach and lodged on his ship as a guest. The two became fast friends and before their parting in late 1717, they had plundered and captured many merchant ships up and down the East Coast.

In June 1718, Blackbeard convinced Bonnet to accept a pardon from North Carolina Governor Charles Eden. This is where Blackbeard and Bonnet parted ways. While Bonnet did accept the pardon and stayed in North Carolina to officially seal the deal, Blackbeard made off with his ship and his plunder. By summer Bonnet, fueled by the betrayal of his friend, returned to piracy.

In September 1718, a naval expedition against pirates began on the river under the authorization of South Carolina Governor Robert Johnson. Stede Bonnet and several others were captured. They were brought to Charleston in early October and were prisoners at the Provost Dungeon. Because of Stede Bonnet's station in life and military service in the past, he was detained at the Warden's house next door. By late October, though, Bonnet had escaped by walking through the front door wearing women's clothing and a wig. He was recaptured on Sullivan's Island and brought to justice on November 10. Bonnet was hanged December 10, 1718 at what is now White Point Gardens.

Many Charleston visitors strolling through the park claim to see the ghost of Stede Bonnet and other pirates who met their fate on the gallows. White Point Gardens was opened in 1837 as a public park. However, during the Civil War the park was fortified to protect the city from union troops. Cannons still line the edges of the park.

THE OLD EXCHANGE AND PROVOST DUNGEON

Of all the fascinating stories I heard while preparing to write this book, no single location had more documented colorful history than that of the Old Exchange and Provost Dungeon.

Ghostly Patriots

As the city exploded with import and export trade, the need for a place to conduct business began to become apparent. After a plea by wealthy merchants and investors to the government, the Old Exchange was built in 1771 to provide a place to conduct both public and private business. The Horlbeck brothers were responsible for the construction of the building.

In 1815, the post office moved to the Exchange Building. By 1847, the first United States postage stamps were sold here. In 1860, South Carolina was the first state to secede from the Union. Through this event, the Confederate postmasters came up with a new postage system. The postmaster invented the five-cent stamp and had it printed and sold. By 1896, the postal service was permanently removed from the Old Exchange building.

Some years ago, a group of teenagers visited the Old Exchange and Provost Dungeon. As they were talking, out of the corner of his eye one of the boys saw what he thought was a man dressed in nostalgic clothing behind the old postmaster's counter. He walked toward the man thinking the old station was being used as an information counter. As he drew near, the man disappeared.

The cellar of the Old Exchange was used as a prison and eventually became known as the "Provost Dungeon." Conditions in the dungeon were less than ideal. It was cold and in places water constantly seeped underfoot and welled up into puddles. With no

The Old Exchange Building and Provost Dungeon, circa 1771.

way to heat the dungeon, several prisoners succumbed to sickness and perished. Others were tortured and died. To the right of the entrance of the dungeon is a pit that glows with a blue hue. This pit was used to store indigo. Underground water constantly seeps into the pit and rumor has it that several prisoners drowned there.

Eight years ago a young man found himself staring out at the ocean just outside Charleston. He had reached a crossroads in his life and was uncertain of where he wanted to settle down. He decided to explore the city. His journey led him to the Old Exchange building where he inquired about the tour. After a short discussion concerning the historical facts, he was led to the Dungeon area; the tour guide then excused himself saying he would "be right back."

Alone in the basement, the young man listened as the mechanical drone as a "canned" tour began. When it stopped abruptly, he was startled. A strange sensation came over him as goose bumps formed on his arms. He had the unmistakable feeling that he was being watched. When he heard footsteps, he turned toward them thinking that the tour guide had returned. Instead, he saw before him the apparition of what he could only describe as a pirate. The figure was wearing brown breeches, a long white vest, and a bandana on his head.

The pirate appeared to be flabbergasted and said, "You aren't alive! I saw them cut your head off!" The young man responded, reassuring the "pirate" that he was, indeed, alive. When he realized that he was carrying on a conversation with a ghost, he fled the building and hasn't been back since.

Tour guides report that the mannequins that are set up within the dungeon move of their own accord. Their heads are often found facing other directions. Rattling chains and the movement of small items throughout the dungeon are not uncommon. As I interviewed Charleston residents concerning the Old Exchange Building and Provost Dungeon, one ex-staff member surprised me with what he had to say.

He was working downstairs, when he heard the sound of voices. Knowing that the building was locked up, he was annoyed thinking someone had somehow gotten in. He climbed the stairs only to find that the building was completely empty. He returned to the dungeon to finish his work. Once again he was interrupted, this time by the sound of piercing screams. Deciding his work was done for the day, he turned to leave. There, between two of the exhibits he witnessed a chain rock back and forth violently. He left the Dungeon and refused to work alone in the building until he retired.

The Sad Story of Isaac Hayne

It's hard to imagine in our world today that seeking medical attention for your family would contribute to being put to death for treason. Isaac Hayne was a decorated Revolutionary War soldier. He also served in the senate and was a prominent Charleston citizen. In 1765, Hayne married Elizabeth Hutson. Together they reared seven children. He owned three plantations just north of Charleston and also partnered with a man named William Hill in the Aera Ironworks Company. The company manufactured ammunition for the use of American forces.

In 1776, Isaac Hayne joined the militia as a Captain and left for Charleston. He returned to his home a few years later. While various rumors persist concerning Hayne and his role in Charleston after the war subsided, one thing is for sure — he would be hanged for treason.

Sometime in 1780, Hayne traveled to Charleston to secure a physician and medication for his family, as they were suffering with smallpox. While he was in the city, he was cornered and questioned concerning his allegiance to Britain. He signed a document under duress proclaiming an oath to the British who were occupying Charleston at the time. By the spring of 1781, Hayne, a true American Patriot, was once again active in the militia against the British. In July, he was captured and, because of the oath he signed while seeking medical care for his family, was charged with treason. Hayne was imprisoned at the Provost Dungeon.

There are reports that the ghost of Isaac Hayne visited his sister's house on a prominent road in downtown Charleston. Historical research provided a detailed and chilling account of his hanging. An excerpt from The Execution of Isaac Hayne by David K. Bowden (Bowden, 1977):

"The streets were crowded with thousands of anxious spectators . . . When the city barrier was past, and the instrument of catastrophe appeared full in view, a faithful friend by his side observed to him, 'that he hoped he would exhibit an example of the manner in which an American can die.' He answered with the utmost tranquility, 'I will endeavor to do so.' He ascended the cart with a firm step and serene aspect. He enquired of the executioner, who was making an attempt to get the cap over his eyes, what he wanted? Upon being informed of his design, the colonel replied, 'I will save you that trouble,' and he pulled it over himself. He was afterwards asked whether he wished to say anything, to which he answered, 'I will only take leave of my friends, and be ready.' He then affectionately shook hands with three gentlemen—recommended his children to their care—and gave the signal for the cart to move."

Legendary tales of the hanging persist today. One story states that his children were present as he was escorted to the gallows on August 4, 1781. The children misinterpreted the procession as a parade and called out to their father. Isaac promised to return to the children if he could. The children were taken to the house of their aunt where she had a woeful conversation with them at bedtime. As she was explaining that their father would never return, she heard the unmistakable sound of his footsteps coming up the stairs. With tremendous hope, she ran to greet her brother who, of course, wasn't there. Many tales of a ghostly encounter with the spirit of Isaac Hayne at his sister's residence were relayed until December 20, 1860. The legend also states that the essence of Isaac Hayne was heartbroken when South Carolina seceded from the Union. The apparition was reportedly never again seen within the home.

However, one visitor to Provost Dungeon is convinced that the spirit of Isaac Hayne has simply moved to another location. An architect from St. Louis entered the Dungeon and stood admiring the building's features. Faintly he heard a raspy voice whisper in his ear, "I am Hayne." He turned around just in time to see a medium built man in his 30's disappear into the wall.

The Old Exchange and Provost Dungeon offers both self-guided and guided tours. They are open seven days a week from 9 a.m. to 5 p.m. For more information, please visit their website at www. oldexchange.com.

THE OLD SLAVE MART MUSEUM

In an unassuming building on Chalmers Street is a museum dedicated to the era of the slave trade in Charleston. In 1856, the Slave Mart was opened for the unimaginable purpose of human slave trade. After the end of the Civil War, the building stood empty until finally being purchased and used for various businesses before once again becoming vacant. In 1973, the building was purchased and placed on the National Register of Historic Places.

The Old Slave Mart Museum, circa 1856.

Julie was ready for the birthday party. All she had to do was wrap the gift. She put the purple bow and wrapping paper on the table along with a roll of tape. She walked to the back room to retrieve a pair of scissors. Frustrated, she opened drawer after drawer in disbelief, but the scissors could not be found.

Deciding to "make due," she returned to the front and realized that the tape had now disappeared. Sure she had placed it on the table, she looked underneath to see if it had fallen. There was nothing there.

Thinking she had taken it with her to search for the scissors, she returned to the back room and once again opened various drawers in frustration. Only now the tape and the scissors couldn't be found. Angry by this point, she stomped back to the front room deciding to wrap the gift on the way to her friend's house. As she gathered her things, she felt a familiar chill and stopped in her tracks.

Julie stood up and faced the doorway to the back room. She couldn't shake the sensation that someone or something wanted her to go back in there. Cautiously, she took a step and called out to "it."

"Okay, I'm coming back in there. Please don't scare me. I don't want to see you."

As Julie entered her office, she turned on the light switch and rubbed her now very cold arms. She walked toward her desk staring in disbelief. There, next to her paper clips, were the scissors and the tape. As Julie approached, she said, "Very funny." But when she saw a dark figure in the reflection of the scissors as she reached for them, Julie screamed.

As I interviewed Julie, she explained that she had seen spectral figures in the small museum building many times before. Although she didn't feel that the ghostly apparitions would harm her, she still didn't like seeing them. She said she often spoke aloud when she sensed their presence and normally they would leave her alone. She said she wondered if this particular spirit was feeling a little mischievous due to the birthday party festivities. Julie speculated that they must long to leave the Old Slave Mart Museum.

The Gullah Legends

During the eighteenth and nineteenth centuries, the slave trade was booming in Charleston. Many slaves were taken from Africa and parts of the Caribbean. They were brought to

Charleston under miserable conditions. Many descendants of those long ago slaves remain in Charleston today. They are known as Gullah or geechie people. Their spiritual traditions have been passed down through the ages.

The Praise House was born from the days before the Civil War when strict plantation owners would not allow slaves to leave their quarters to attend church. A little known law from that dark time stated that the bodies of human slaves could be owned, but their souls could not. Therefore, slaveholders could disallow their slaves from leaving the plantation grounds, but had no choice but to allow them to worship on the property.

Enterprising slaves designated unoccupied shacks as the Praise House and would meet there for worship. Music was important to the congregation and the Praise House was usually the only place where slaves could chant or sing their native songs. Although several Praise Houses are still in existence today, the historic buildings are rarely used for worship.

One such praise house exists to this day at Boone Hall Plantation. The slaves built that Praise House using bricks that were manufactured at the plantation. Several tour guides and other staff members report hearing the lofty sounds of singing coming from inside the building.

The leader of the Praise House was usually looked upon as a mystic. He was usually a medicine man who officiated over weddings and funerals and gave spiritual advice. When the sick or injured could not make it to the Praise House, he would visit and carry the "spirit" to them.

Haint Blue

The Gullah people incorporated spiritual beliefs with legendary stories of ghosts, which they refer to as "haints." A haint is defined as a spirit of the dead who has not moved on from the physical world. To keep haints from inhabiting their home, Gullah people would paint the wood blue around their doors and windows. The exact color of blue varied depending on the pigmentations that were available. Therefore, there is no "true haint blue." Ceilings were also painted with the color in the hopes of keeping the home safe. The painted ceilings were also thought to confuse insects into thinking the ceiling was the sky. A drive through some parts of Charleston and especially along the coastal islands will afford a curious onlooker picture perfect homes with "haint blue" painted doors.

Plat Eyes

The Gullah people believe that Plat Eyes is a prowling ghost that can change its appearance for any purpose it sees fit. This ghost is believed to be that of departed spirits that wander the earth. Typically, the ghost presents itself as an animal. It can change forms at will and has been known to kill. Gullah people try to avoid being outside between twilight and dawn, as this is the time most likely that one might encounter a Plat Eyes. Legend states that this ghost cannot stand the smell of gunpowder or sulphur.

The Gullah people have had interesting ceremonies to prevent a departed loved one from returning as a Plat Eyes. Typically at a wake or funeral, the guests are served coffee. Each guest pours a small amount onto the ground as an offering. When the time for burial comes, the guests lay face down. Once the dearly departed has been lowered into the grave, the Gullah people rise up and drum, sing, and dance. The ceremony is not complete until all the mourners have tossed a handful of dirt into the grave. The graves of the dearly departed are typically adorned with possessions. Removing anything from a Gullah grave is said to bring terrible bad luck.

Boo Hag

Boo Hags are creatures that seek to steal energy from unsuspecting victims. Boo Hags will steal the skin of their intended victim so that they can pass themselves off as old women during the daylight hours. In wearing the skin, they can disguise themselves and move among the living freely while searching for a new victim. The body of a Boo Hag (without skin) is said to be blood red. The eyes are red as well. Because they have no skin, they feel like raw meat and are always warm to the touch. They are also slippery and difficult to catch and hold.

When a Boo Hag finds a victim, she waits until nightfall. The Boo Hag will shed its skin and perch on the chest of their sleeping victim. There, they will begin to suck their breath away. This is called "riding." As the Boo Hag "rides" their victim, he/she slips into a dream state, paralyzing them and leaving them helpless.

Should the victim wake and begin to struggle, the Boo Hag will simply steal their skin. If the victim sleeps through the incident, there is nothing to show for the strange attack in the morning other than feeling very tired and, well, drained.

The Gullah people have also passed down the tradition of handweaving sea grass baskets. During the slavery era, the baskets were made for agricultural purposes. Later, they were made and utilized for every day living. As slavery and the plantation way of life began to dwindle, former slaves began making and selling the sea grass baskets as a method of income. Some time around the early twentieth century there was resurgence in the art and sea grass baskets were once again in great demand.

Today, you can visit the Market Place in Charleston to see the basket weavers in action. The baskets are incredible, intricately woven pieces of art. Because they are made of sea grass, water will not hurt them. One basket weaver told me that her baskets were dishwasher safe and will maintain their shape for years. During my visits to Charleston, I did notice that sea grass baskets are much like everything else — you get what you pay for. The open market is a great place to buy the hand-crafted baskets, however, attractions outside the historic district also showcase the craft and usually at discounted prices.

Storytelling

Gullah people speak an English-based Creole language. Examples are: chillun (children); 'leb'n (eleven); cootuh (turtle), and buckruh (white man). They also have a rich storytelling history. Joel Chandler Harris wrote many stories taken directly from the Gullah people. His stories are legendary. Compiling several stories from the Gullah people, Mr. Harris published them into a book called Legends of the Old Plantations (Harris, 1881). This is "Tar-Baby."

TAR-BABY

"Didn't the fox never catch the rabbit, Uncle Remus?" asked the little boy the next evening.

"He come mighty nigh it, honey, sho's you born—Brer Fox did. One day atter Brer Rabbit fool 'im wid dat calamus root, Brer Fox went ter wuk en got 'im some tar, en mix it wid some turkentime, en fix up a contrapshun w'at he call a Tar-Baby, en he tuck dish yer Tar-Baby en he sot 'er in de big road, en den he lay off in de bushes fer to see what de news wuz gwine ter be. En he didn't hatter wait long, nudder, kaze bimeby here come Brer Rabbit pacin' down de road — lippity-clippity, clippity, lippity — dez ez sassy ez a jay-bird. Brer Fox, he lay low. Brer Rabbit come prancin' 'long twel he spy de Tar-Baby, en den he fotch up on his behime legs like he wuz 'stonished. De Tar Baby, she sot dar, she did, en Brer Fox, he lay low.

"'Mawnin'!' sez Brer Rabbit, sezee — 'nice wedder dis mawnin',' sezee.

"Tar-Baby ain't sayin' nuthin', en Brer Fox he lay low.

"'How duz yo' sym'tums seem ter segashuate?' sez Brer Rabbit, sezee.

"Brer Fox, he wink his eye slow, en lay low, en de Tar-Baby, she ain't sayin' nuthin'.

"'How you come on, den? Is you deaf?' sez Brer Rabbit, sezee. 'Kaze if you is, I kin holler louder,' sezee.

"Tar-Baby stay still, en Brer Fox, he lay low.

"'You er stuck up, dat's w'at you is,' says Brer Rabbit, sezee, 'en I'm gwine ter kyore you, dat's w'at I'm a gwine ter do,' sezee.

"Brer Fox, he sorter chuckle in his stummick, he did, but Tar-Baby ain't sayin' nothin'.

"'I'm gwine ter larn you how ter talk ter 'spectubble folks ef hit's de las' ack,' sez Brer Rabbit, sezee. 'Ef you don't take off dat hat en tell me howdy, I'm gwine ter bus' you wide open,' sezee.

"Tar-Baby stay still, en Brer Fox, he lay low.

"Brer Rabbit keep on axin' 'im, en de Tar-Baby, she keep on sayin' nothin', twel present'y Brer Rabbit draw back wid his fis', he did, en blip he tuck 'er side er de head. Right dar's whar he broke his merlasses jug. His fis' stuck, en he can't pull loose. De tar hilt 'im. But Tar-Baby, she stay still, en Brer Fox, he lay low.

"'Ef you don't lemme loose, I'll knock you agin,' sez Brer Rabbit, sezee, en wid dat he fotch 'er a wipe wid de udder han', en dat stuck. Tar-Baby, she ain'y sayin' nuthin', en Brer Fox, he lay low.

"'Tu'n me loose, fo' I kick de natal stuffin' outen you,' sez Brer Rabbit, sezee, but de Tar-Baby, she ain't sayin' nuthin'. She des hilt on, en de Brer Rabbit lose de use er his feet in de same way. Brer Fox, he lay low. Den Brer Rabbit squall out dat ef de Tar-Baby don't tu'n 'im loose he butt 'er cranksided. En den he butted, en his head got stuck. Den Brer Fox, he sa'ntered fort', lookin' dez ez innercent ez wunner yo' mammy's mockin'-birds.

"'Howdy, Brer Rabbit,' sez Brer Fox, sezee. 'You look sorter stuck up dis mawnin',' sezee, en den he rolled on de groun', en laft en laft twel he couldn't laff no mo'. 'I speck you'll take dinner wid me dis time, Brer Rabbit. I done laid in some calamus root, en I ain't gwineter take no skuse,' sez Brer Fox, sezee."

Here Uncle Remus paused, and drew a two-pound yam out of the ashes.

"Did the fox eat the rabbit?" asked the little boy to whom the story had been told.

"Dat's all de fur de tale goes," replied the old man. "He mout, an den agin he moutent. Some say Judge B'ar come 'long en loosed 'im — some say he didn't. I hear Miss Sally callin'. You better run 'long."

While controversy surrounded some of Harris' works and the subsequent Disney movie "Song of the South," he remained true to the stories as they were told to him by the low country Gullah people. Incidentally, his home is now a house museum in Atlanta. His great-great-great-grandson, Lain Shakespeare, is its executive director and it's dubbed "The Wren's Nest" and is open to the public. Mr. Harris' bedroom remains untouched and has been left as it was on the day of his death. The house is reportedly haunted and I have had the privilege of investigating there several times. The Wren's Nest is worth a visit. For more information, please visit www.wrensnestonline.com.

Chapter Ten:

OTHER ANOMALIES

UFO REPORTS IN CHARLESTON

There have been times during my research when the individual relaying paranormal events tells a very different kind of story. Usually the client will sheepishly describe intense feelings of being watched and followed by seeing something they can't explain, such as bright blinding lights in the night sky or worse...small alien creatures.

Abducted by Aliens

Angela sat on the sofa across from me as she described the events that took place in her home more than three years ago. She began by telling me that she experienced a "normal and happy childhood." She had graduated high school with honors and went on to earn a Bachelor of Technology degree from Charleston Southern University. She was married once, but sadly her husband was killed in a car accident only two years after their wedding. Angela had no children and lived alone in Charleston, working as a bank manager.

As Angela drove home one evening after work, she couldn't shake the feeling that she was being watched. She walked in the door and went about her usual routine of making something to eat before settling in to watch a TV show before going to bed. Still, she couldn't shake the feeling. When she finally snuggled into bed, the feeling had become quite nagging.

Angela was dreaming. In her dream, she was watching herself sleep in her bedroom. Outside a strange light was casting a blue haze on the bedroom walls and in the blue haze there was a small humanoid creature. It was moving cautiously toward Angela's sleeping form. Her dream self's view changed and suddenly she could see the outline of the creature's face. She described it as being triangular in shape with a very small mouth and huge oversized slanted eyes. The nose was very tiny indeed and the nostrils were mere slits. In her dream state Angela saw the creature turn toward the window. It "spoke" in a myriad of clicks and whistles. The sounds were not audible, but Angela described them as being telepathically "heard."

The creature turned back toward Angela and reached out a four-fingered hand. It touched her cheek with an icy finger and suddenly Angela found herself standing in a strange room. The walls were gray. The floor appeared to be white and opaque. Angela marveled at how warm the floor felt on her bare feet. All around her small creatures were coming in and out of the room. Some of them stopped to look at her and she sensed them telepathically trying to reassure her. Angela was being led to a small metal table. There, she was asked to lie down. As one of the smaller creatures moved closer, Angela saw that it was holding a long, sharp scalpel.

Her arms became unbearably heavy and she found herself unable to move. The taller creature reassured her yet again and Angela watched as the smaller alien made an incision in her arm. Angela fainted. Some time later she opened her eyes to find herself back in her own bed in her bedroom. There was no more blue hue and certainly no more tiny creatures from outer space. At first, she believed it all really had been a dream. She went into the kitchen to get a glass of water, and as she reached for a bottle of water from the refrigerator, she saw a small, fresh incision on her right arm. Angela still bears a scar today.

Hovering Craft

While alien abductions seem to be rare, UFO sightings are not uncommon in Charleston. Several accounts of bright lights and hovering craft have been reported throughout the years. One such report was in the early 1990s.

Eric, an eight-year-old boy, and his father, Bruce, were on the way back home after visiting family on a nearby island. The country road was dark and it was getting late. In the distance, a single bright light appeared on the roadway ahead. The light was so bright that the young son inquired about what kind of vehicle it might be. At first, Bruce thought it was a motorcycle. When he realized it was traveling toward them faster than any motorcycle could travel, he slowed his own vehicle down and eventually stopped.

The single-lighted craft whirred by them at lightning speed. Inside the car, father and son stared at each other. When Bruce finally spoke, he tried dismissing the vehicle as obviously some kind of 'test car.' "Cool!" Eric said. As Bruce took his foot off the brake and applied it to the gas pedal, the car engine made a sputtering noise and then suddenly stopped. He turned the key, becoming increasingly frustrated as the engine refused to crank. In the rear view mirror, a dim light appeared. Within seconds, it grew in intensity as the now panicking driver realized that the object was heading back towards them.

The craft approached the vehicle and hovered above them. Bright light cascaded into the car and the young father, never taking his eyes off the craft, quietly instructed his son to move onto the floorboard and to remain very still. As Eric complied, the craft gained altitude, moving to about twenty feet in front of the car. The whirring noise became louder and louder and the craft took off into the night sky. After regaining his composure, the shaken father reached for his son, pulling him up from the floorboard and back onto the seat. The youngster smiled and patted his father on the arm. "It's okay, Daddy. That was so cool!" Father and son arrived safely home.

Bruce and Eric's story was baffling... more baffling is the fact that on that very same night several Charlestonians reported seeing unusual lights in the night sky.

Lights in the Sky

Bruce's story was eerily reminiscent to another account. I came across a personal experience that was written by a young woman named Jessica. I promptly contacted her and this is her written account:

"I live in Charleston, SC...a state that's well known for its ghosts! Well, I hadn't really seen many before, even though I knew I lived in a city that was rich with a history of ghosts... my friend one day told me about the "lights of Ravanel," where, down this dark road in Ravanel, there are unexplainable lights when one drives. I didn't really take him seriously... until I went with him.

We drove a long way out, to a highway that had trees all along it, and hardly any lampposts. Ravanel is basically country land... we took a turn onto a small road into a neighborhood called "Parks Ferry." Michael started speeding down the road and suddenly there was this single red orb-light right in the middle of the street ahead of us... not a car!! Michael exclaimed that it had come out extremely early and he was very excited. However, I was scared! Now, this road has only one lamppost that is in the middle of the long road. This was neither a car nor a lamppost! It was this solemn red orb that kept coming near to our speeding car and then dashing away ahead of us... Completely unexplainable! Then suddenly, it disappeared! By that point, I was flipping out... I had never seen a Charleston spirit before and this was just too much for me... The road was completely dark and I was just scared.

> So after the red light disappeared... Mike turned the car around, and headed back down the road. Then the SECOND lights appeared and Mike got excited again! This time, they were three white lights piled on top of each other... made no sense whatsoever! They were NOT cars, or anything, just these weird lights that appeared right after the red, down the opposite direction of the road.... We chased after those too, and again, we would seem to catch up to those lights, but then they would zip off ahead of us... keeping shy of being caught. Then, they disappeared!!! I started crying... and begged to go back home. The lights had completely freaked me out!"

Gravity Hill

Initially, I thought that perhaps the lights were seen in the distance. Geographical anomalies can certainly cause all sorts of illusions. Car lights from many miles away combined with these geographical anomalies can create the optical illusion that disembodied lights are much closer. But, I have no explanation (aside from the possibility of our government testing top secret aircraft) for the lights that hover only a few feet from the witnesses.

Anti-gravity hills are also perfect examples of geographical anomalies being portrayed as paranormal events. We've all heard the story...

> A bunch of teenagers are swapping scary stories when one of them mentions that there's an old road (usually just out of town) where, when a vehicle is placed in neutral at the bottom of the hill, it will mysteriously roll up the hill. This is normally followed with an "explanation" involving a tragic car accident in which children were killed. Usually the teens will head out to said deserted road and give it a try. Most of the stories end with the ghostly handprints of the accident victims being discovered on the back of the vehicle.

I live a stone's throw from one such anti gravity hill in the Atlanta area. Our anti gravity hill is linked to the lynching of an innocent man, as the "hanging tree" still stands today in close proximity to the bottom of the hill. The handprints are supposedly the victim's relatives attempting to push people away from the area.

If you're going to test an anti gravity hill for yourself, I recommend that you first wash and thoroughly dry the back of your car and grab some baby powder before heading out. If the car truly seems "pushed," baby powder can be used to dust for handprints.

CRYPTOZOOLOGY

Cryptozoology literally means the study of hidden animals. In the paranormal world, the definition is the study of creatures whose existence is unknown. There are many well-known cryptozoological creatures such as the Loch Ness monster. The Chubacabra, Big Foot, and the Jersey Devil are other well-known cryptozoological creatures.

Woodland Creature

Several residents in and around the rural areas of Charleston had been perplexed concerning the sighting of a strange animal. In the early morning hours in April, Scott was getting ready for work. Outside his dogs were beginning to bark. Scott had always enjoyed living in the country and had become accustomed to the dogs barking at a wandering turkey or other woodland creatures, but on this day something was different.

As he poured his morning coffee, he realized that the dogs had begun to whine and bark more furiously. He opened the back door and, as he did, he caught a glimpse of something grey moving just beyond the yard in the thicket. The dogs were watching it too... Whatever it was, it moved quickly and quietly.

Scott put down his coffee and took the steps down the back porch into the yard. He remembered something his sister said about hairless foxes and wanted to get a good look at whatever it was. As he moved slowly, the dogs settled down. From their pen, they watched Scott move ever so carefully closer to the creature that was now crouching behind a thick group of bushes. Scott took another step and the animal sprang from its hiding place.

Although it seemed to be about the size of a fox, this creature was unlike anything Scott had ever seen. It growled at him, took a step backward, and suddenly leapt into the woods and disappeared. Scott described the animal as having the face of a cat, but the body was more like a dog. The creature's fur appeared to be very short, but in some places, particularly around the neck and ankles, it was long and wispy. The most prominent feature by far was the eyes.

"They were dark and, when it was looking at me, I felt like it could see right through me," Scott said.

Scott still lives in the same house bordered by woodlands. He is married now and expecting his first child in November. Scott said he has never seen the creature again, but neighbors reported seeing the same half-cat/half-dog creature. The last reports were in 2007. Residents speculate that the creature is either dead or has been captured.

Mermaid in the Harbor

Tales of mermaids living in the Charleston Harbor date back as early as the 1700s. One such story was relayed in the book Doctor to the Dead, written by John Bennett and first published in 1943. The story relays the account of a flood in the city of Charleston in July 1867. According to the story, the Gullah people believed that the flood was caused by the Sea King who was searching for a missing mermaid whom he believed was being held captive somewhere in the city. Eventually an apothecary on King Street was blamed for holding the mermaid captive and wary citizens stormed the shop. The rain immediately stopped and the sky cleared. The apothecary proclaimed his innocence, which was suddenly a non-issue. Relieved, Charleston citizens assumed that the mermaid made her escape out the back door.

Jim has been fishing off the South Carolina coast for decades. On this particular morning, he had a lot on his mind. His oldest son was serving his last three months in the United States Army on a tour in Iraq. His youngest daughter had given him the news only the night before that she was pregnant. She was married and not living at home, but he couldn't shake a foreboding feeling. His wife attempted to reassure him, to no avail.

As he double-checked the bait, he saw something large moving just below the surface of the water. At first, he thought it was a dolphin, but when it swam by again, he clearly saw a shimmering teal green tail shaped like that of a whale. Stunned, Jim took a step back, quietly sat down, and watched the water. When a mermaid jumped breaking the surface, her long blonde hair glistening in the summer sun, she gracefully swished her teal green tail before disappearing again below the waves. Jim shook his head in disbelief.

Jim sat back down convinced that his distracted mind had misinterpreted a fish, when he heard something hit the side of his boat. Leaning over, he saw the quick swish of the green tail again. This time he was sure that he had really lost his mind, so he decided to head to shore and get to the doctor right away for a full checkup. At the doctor's office, Jim explained what he had seen that morning in the harbor. When the doctor realized that Jim was serious, he stopped laughing and ordered some tests. When all the tests were normal, the doctor sent Jim home to get some rest with instructions to call him should anything else unusual occur.

Jim took some time off from fishing. The unusual creature he had witnessed swimming in the harbor that morning had frightened him enough to keep him landlocked. It was only after the birth of his beautiful twin granddaughters that he decided to return to the boat. As the girls grew, they developed a love for the ocean and truly enjoyed going with grandpa on his fishing trips.

One bright summer morning, the seven-year-old girls excitedly boarded their grandfather's fishing boat. As they headed out into the Charleston harbor, the girls were discussing all sorts of fish. Jim was listening to the girls as they rambled on. As little girls do, it wasn't long before they were discussing the possibility of merpeople. Knowing that what he had witnessed in the harbor years ago was a figment of his imagination, Jim decided not to mention it to the girls.

Jim dropped the anchor and was busy bringing out the bait to ready the fishing poles when he heard one of the girls squeal. Turning his attention toward them, he caught a glimpse of the familiar teal green tail just before it disappeared beneath the surface. Jim resigned to the fact that there was, indeed, a mermaid living in the Charleston Harbor. He has continued various fishing trips with several family members who have been privy to sightings of the magical and mythical creature.

AFTERWORD

I have felt honored and privileged to investigate the paranormal activity throughout Charleston. The city is steeped in mystery and new experiences seem to be recorded every day. Should my readers have the opportunity to visit this magnificent city, I would encourage them to take the not-so-beaten paths and visit some of the historic locations in and around the Holy City. I would also encourage my readers to do some investigating of their own. With the prevalence of paranormal activity that permeates Charleston, surely new stories are waiting to be told.

BIBLIOGRAPHY

Telephone and E-mail Interviews

Bailey Jr., Ralph: VP Brockington & Associates, www.brockington. org.

Ball, Bobbie: Owner, Poogan's Porch. www.poogansporch.com.

Collier, Jim: General Manager, Boone Hall Plantation. www. boonehallplantation.com.

LaVerne, John: Owner, Bulldog Tours. www.bulldogtours.com.

Macy, Edward: Author of The Ghosts of Charleston

Sharpe, Bill: WCSC-TV News Anchor

Sinclair, Rebel: Owner, Black Cat Tours. www.blackcattours.com/ rebel.html.

Youmans, Tony: Facility Manager, Old Exchange and Provost Dungeon. www.oldexchange.com.

Personal Interviews

Brown, Suzann: Tour Guide, Bulldog Tours.

Connor, Sean: Manager, Mad River Grille. www.madrivercharleston. com.

Cooper, Kelly: Manager, Bocci's Italian Restaurant. www.boccis. com.

Edgar, Judi: Tour Guide, Boone Hall Plantation.

Forrester, Cathy: Author of At Home Charleston, www. athomecharleston.com.

Friends of the Hunley, www.hunley.org.

Historic Charleston Foundation, www.historiccharleston.org.

Lawton, Carol: Manager, Tommy Condon's Irish Pub. www. tommycondons.com.

Miller, Ruth: Author of Charleston's Old Exchange Building; A Witness to American History.

Mr. Javanino: Owner, Pizzaria Di Giovanni's.

Parham, Christopher: Manager, Dock Street Theatre.

Sensenbaugh, Abbey: Operations and Tour Manager, Boone Hall Plantation.

Stiles, Dennis: Tour Guide, Low Country Ghost Walk. www.oldcharlestontours.com.

Vandhorst, Isaac: Chef, Poogan's Porch.

Williams, Ginger: Tour Guide, Bulldog Tours.

Book Research

Bennett, John. *Doctor to the Dead.* New York, New York: Rinehart & Company, 1946. Reprinted: Columbia, South Carolina: University of South Carolina Press, 1995.

Bowden, David K. *The Execution of Isaac Hayne.* Lexington, South Carolina: The Sandlapper Store, Inc., 1977.

Brown, Suzann. *A Brief History Revealed: The Old Jail & Prison Camp.* Charleston, South Carolina: self-published, 2008.

Buxton, Geordie. *Haunted Plantations; Ghosts of Slavery and Legends of the Cotton Kingdoms.* Charleston, South Carolina: Arcadia Publishing, 2007.

Harris, Joel Chandler. *Uncle Remus, Legends of the Old Plantations.* New York, New York: D. Appleton & Company, 1880.

Martin, Margaret Rhett. *Charleston Ghosts.* Columbia, South Carolina: University of Columbia Press, 1963.

INDEX